A Darned Good Time

by Miss Lucy Potter
age 13

Taylor, New York
Cortland County
January 26, 1868 - January 29, 1869

New York History Review Press
Elmira, New York

A Darned Good Time

by Miss Lucy Potter, 1868

transcribed by Diane Janowski

Copyright © 2009 Diane Janowski

Published by New York History Review Press

Elmira, New York

For the latest on New York History Review, please visit
www.NewYorkHistoryReview.com

This book was designed and laid out in Adobe InDesign using typeface Adobe Garamond Pro.

ISBN: 978-0-578-02494-3

First Edition

Printed in the United States of America

For Velma, Lafa, and Herbie

Table of Contents

Foreward..8

People in this Diary...12

A Darned Good Time...15

What Happened to Them?......................................137

Afterward...139

Bibliography..141

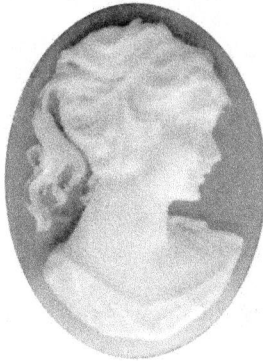

Foreward

In our *Learning from History* series of Upstate New York diaries, accounts of young people's lives on the farm, or in the home, help us to understand their thoughts and experiences. Each narrative offers a unique perspective on teenage life in rural New York, and serves as an important primary resource in the study of American history.

A Darned Good Time is the diary of thirteen-year-old Lucy Jane Potter of Taylor, New York - near Cortland. Beginning on January 26, 1868, Lucy recorded the events of her life in a small (2.25 x 3.5 inches) pocket diary with three entries to the page in very small handwriting. When she filled up the diary at the end of 1868, she started writing over the top of the previous entries for several weeks in 1869. Lucy lived with, and cared for, a disabled aunt about a quarter mile from her childhood home. Back home she had a father, a new stepmother (her mother died seven years earlier) two sisters, and a brother.

Lucy was generally very happy in her life – she enjoyed her family and friends, and going to school and church. In her words she exclaimed love for a boy of twenty-two, and she mentioned him frequently in her diary, although at some point she methodically crossed out most entries about him. Those entries are still somewhat visible.

Lucy's notations were confined to the spaces allotted and are written in pencil with a few in ink. Her handwriting is mostly legible, except for the accounts that were crossed out, and a few names or places that can't be deciphered. Lucy's spelling is left as she spelled it. Clarifications have been added in brackets. The photographed pages from her diary are actual size.

A Darned Good Time invites us into the daily life of a New York teenager through her own words and experiences. We hear Lucy's voice as she shares her joys, sorrows, and enthusiasm for life in a rural farming community.

The Eleanor Barnes Library acquired Lucy Potter's diary in 2008. So far as is known, this transcription is its first published version.

Diane Janowski, Publisher
New York History Review

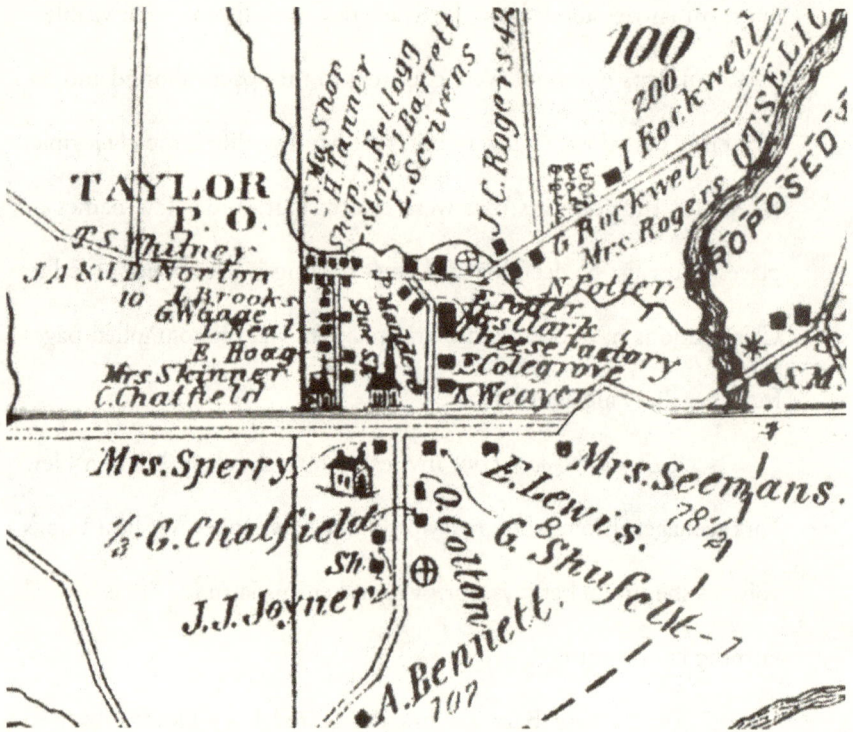

The town of Taylor, New York in 1876. "Mrs. Seemans" is Lucy's Aunt Lucy Seamans. E. Potter is Lucy's father [Edmund Potter].

Taylor, New York today. It measures ¼ mile from Aunt Lucy's farm to Edmund Potter's house. The cheese factory building is still standing.

People in this diary

Lucy's Family in 1868

Edmund Potter - merchant, postmaster, age 37, first wife was
Lillis
Jane Potter - stepmother, age 42
Lafa [Lafrenza] Potter, younger sister, age 8
Velma Potter - older sister, age 15
Herbert Potter - younger brother, age 7
Sarah Seamans Rogers - age 29, cousin
Uncle Noel Seamans - age 70, farmer (young Lucy lived with
the Seamans)
Jerome Seamans - cousin, teacher, age 28
Jane Seamans - cousin, age 22
Aunt Lucy [Potter] Seamans - age 59, married to Noel

Friends and Relations in 1868

Anna and Mercell
Aunt Em (maybe Emiline Seamans)
Aunt Betsy Hayes - age 35
Aunt Hulda
Aunt Leib
Aunt Betsy
Aunt Dorcas (James, Jarner?)
Albert Ellis
Uncle Edwin Hayes - carpenter, age 36
Aunt Lizzie and Minnie
Bart (Barton) {Roark] - age 24, laborer - lived in Homer, NY
Bill Andrews - age 19, farmer
Francis Barnes
Sophia Bennett - friend of Jerome
Sarah Bennett - age 34
Mr. Bennett [Alfred] - farmer, age 35
Uncle Amos [Bowen] - farmer, age 61

Aunt Philander or Phylinda [Bowen] - age 54
George Chatfield - age 16
Mrs. Chatfield
Mrs. [Mary] Chatfield - age 42
Abb [Albert Clark] - age 22, the boy Lucy loved, lived in town
Milo Clark
Miss Collins
Nick Cyrus
Carrie Cline
Denton [Dent] (James, Jarner?) age 18, cousin
Delett and Edith
Dewit
Josephine Gilmore
George Guage - age 21, shoemaker, neighbor
Mrs. Hakes
Mr. [John] Harrison - age 75, farmer, lived next door to Seamans
Hoag (maybe Edwin Hoag)
Mrs. Holeroid (Hollenbeck?)
Mrs. Holmes
Mr. Hoyes
Hut - Andrew Hutchinson, age 61, farmer
Mary Hutchinson - age 16, neighbor
Jaleana
Ed Knapp - age 20, farm laborer
[Mr.] Lock - ran a hotel in town and grew hops
Mrs. Loomis
Lunise and Amelia
Mrs. McGanner
Mrs. McLaughlin
Minnie Monroe - married to Orin
Nancy
Frank Neal
Mrs. Neal - age 45, neighbor
Osphia [probably Sophia Bennett]
Mr. Osborn/Mrs. Osborn
Oscar and wife
Ellen [Emma?] Pendleton
Dora Potter - age 8, cousin, sister of Rose

Frank Potter - age 11, cousin
Aunt Harriet Potter - age 49
Mina Potter - age 11, cousin
Minor Potter - age 10, cousin
Orvil Potter - age 18, cousin
Nelson Potter - age 45, uncle, farm laborer
Rosa/Rose Potter - age 14, cousin, sister of Dora
Mrs. Rathbone
Mrs. Pritchard/Prichard
Ellie Pritchard
Mrs. Wrechkell (Rockwell)
Lizzie Rockwell
Mrs. Rogers (Lavena) - neighbor
Julius Seamans - age 40, relative, drover, lived in East Virgil, New York
Sarah Seamans - age 80
Emmes [Elizabeth] Sergent
Lu [Lewis?] Sergent
Mr. [George] Shufelt - age 28, lived next door to Harrisons
Silvernail - farmer
the Silvernail girls
Mrs. Smith
Mrs. Tanner
Uncle Will Watson - age 21, farmer
Aunt Lydia Watson - age 17
Mr. & Mrs. Wentworth
Almira [Amelia] West - wife of Joseph
Inez West - age 11
Mr. West
Uncle John Wheeler- age 61, farmer, lived in Solon, New York
Aunt Sarah Wheeler - age 55
Mr. [Thadeus] Whitney - lived next door to Lucy's parents
Mr. & Mrs. Wise
Mary Wise

A Darned Good Time

(1868 starts on January 26, 1868)

January, Sunday 26, 1868

I got [up] this morning. It was snowing. It has snowed all day. I went to Church this forenoon, but did not go this evening.

January, Monday 27, 1868

We have been washing tonight. I have not done much this afternoon. did not go to School today.

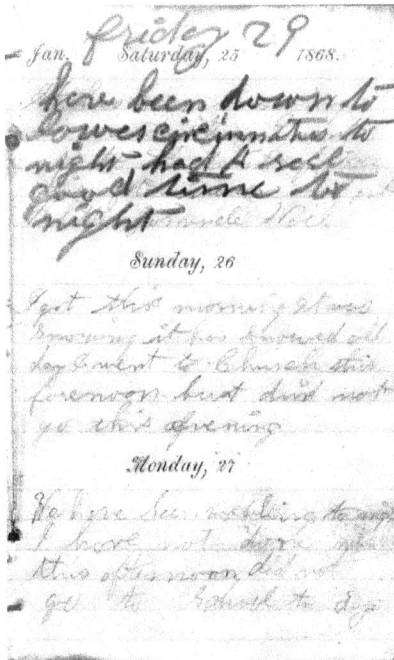

January, Tuesday 28, 1868
Jane has gone to funrel of Mr. ---- Whitney. Buriel today.
Carrie Cline and Mr. Osborn has been here today.

January, Wednesday 29, 1868
I got up this morning and it was storming like everything.
this afternoon I went up to the post office and had lots of
fun.

January, Thursday 30, 1868
Aunt Em staid here last Night and she went home this forenoon. Aunt Lucy, Sarah, Jane, went up to Uncle ------ this
afternoon.

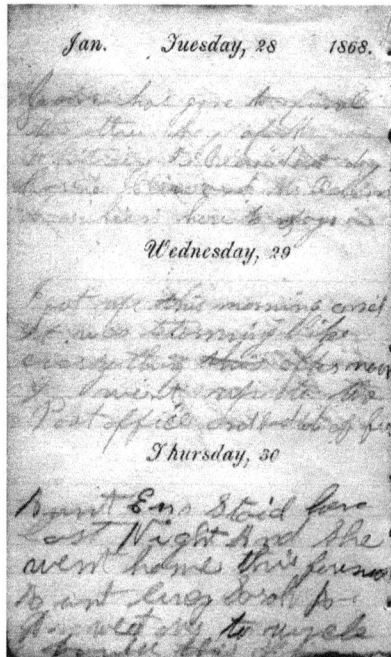

January, Friday 31, 1868
I got up this morning and help[ed] get the work out of the way. Aunt Lucy got A letter from Jerome tonight.

February, Saturday 1, 1868
F got up this Morning found it was very pleasant. this afternoon I went up to Pa's and tonight Velma and Lafa came home to [too].

February, Sunday 2, 1868
I did not go to meeting this forenoon but this girls went this Evening. I went to Meeting.

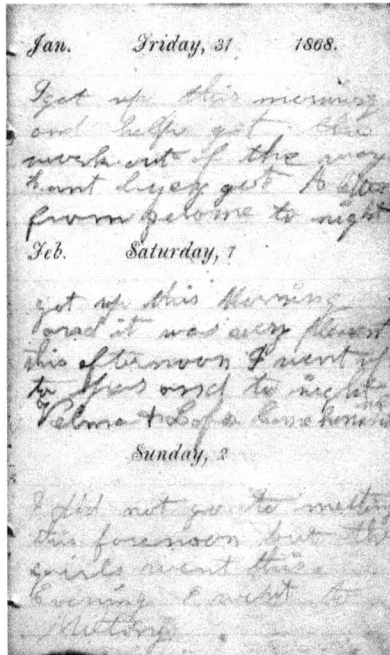

February, Monday 3, 1868
I got up this morning and helped get the work out of the way.

February, Tuesday 4, 1868
I helped get the work out of the way and went up to Pa's this afternoon and had my hair curled.

February, Wednesday 5, 1868
I went up to Mr. Hoyes' last night to the party and had a very good time. got home about 3 o'clock.

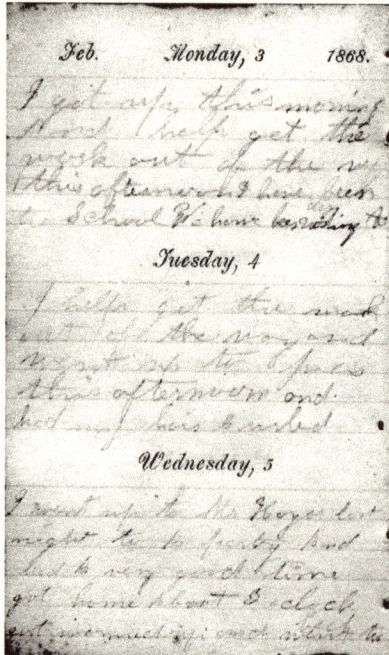

February, Thursday 6, 1868
got up this morning it was snowing like the DEVIL and blowing and drifting like everything. We have been to baking all day.

February, Friday 7, 1868
It has been snowing and blowing like everything. It is not very good going. We have not been eny where today.

February, Saturday 8, 1868
It is quite pleasant today. I have been over to Uncle John's today and had a real good time. Jennie Potter is not only [dead] but Alive.

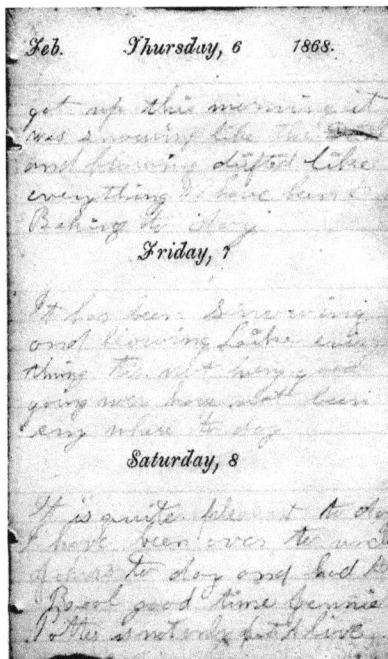

February, Sunday 9, 1868
I went to Church today - there was not a great many there. I went in the evening too and it was pretty bad.

February, Monday 10, 1868
we have been washing today - did not go up to the post office.

February, Tuesday 11, 1868
have been to Jennie Potter's funrel today. She look real Natural. Come home. Em S-- come here tonight.

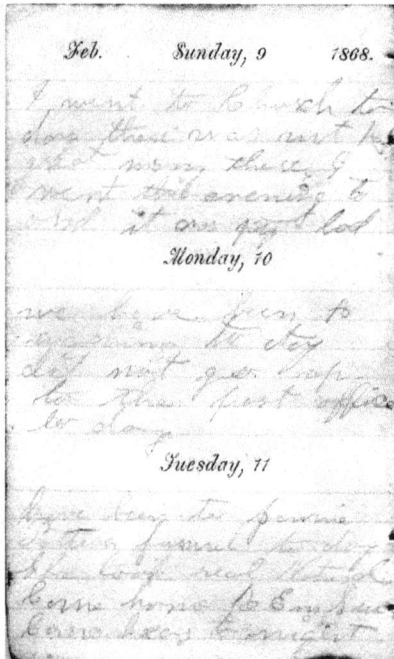

February, Wednesday 12, 1868
I got up this morning and helped get the work out of the way.

February, Thursday 13, 1868
we have been baking today. I went up to the store this forenoon and this afternoon I went to the field [?].

February, Friday 14, 1868
George Guage has been down and got Jerome today. Aunt Em has been over here today. Pa has picked out --- -----.

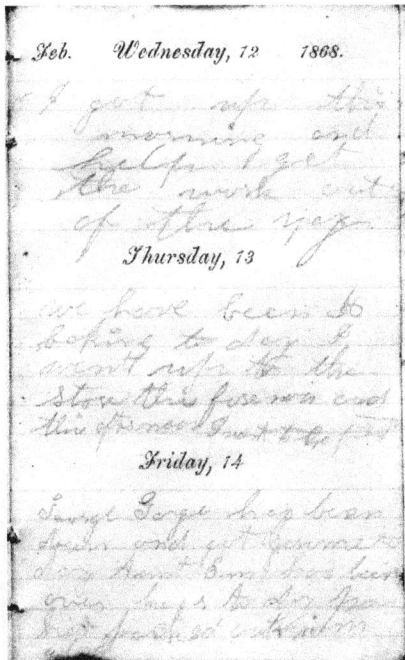

February, Saturday 15, 1868
we got the work out of the way about 1 o'clock. Dewit and Francis Barnes come but they went up to Mr. Whitney's this evening. went to bed about 9 o'clock.

February, Sunday 16, 1868
I did not go to Church today. Dewit and Frank went home today -----Aunt Em and Jane [and] i went to Meeting - so did Velma.

February, Monday 17, 1868
We have been working today. It snows like everything. Sarah and i went out and got through and went in clear up to my knees.

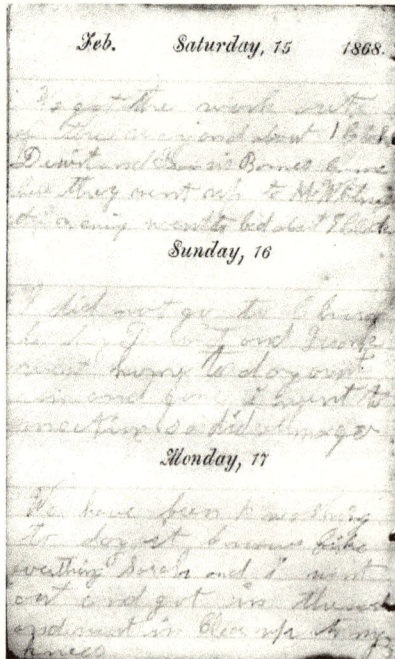

February, Tuesday 18, 1868
got the work out of the way & Aunt Philanda Vesronsler Potter & Albert B---came. Em Sarah, and Jane and Em went to the post office.

February, Wednesday 19, 1868
I have been to school today, Jane, Sarah has gone up to Union Valley.

February, Thursday 20, 1868
I have been to school today. Mrs. Rathbone is buried this afternoon. Carrie & Rose is here. Aunt Em is here.

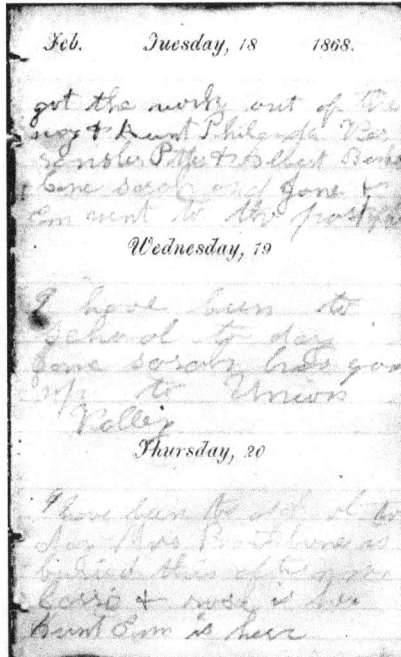

February, Friday 21, 1868
i have been to school today. There is a party down to Clines
- And Lafa left to school to [too].

February, Saturday 22, 1868
this forenoon I went up to the store. Carrie Cline has been
here this evening. I have had a darned good time.

February, Sunday 23, 1868
I have not felt very well today. Abb is here tonight.

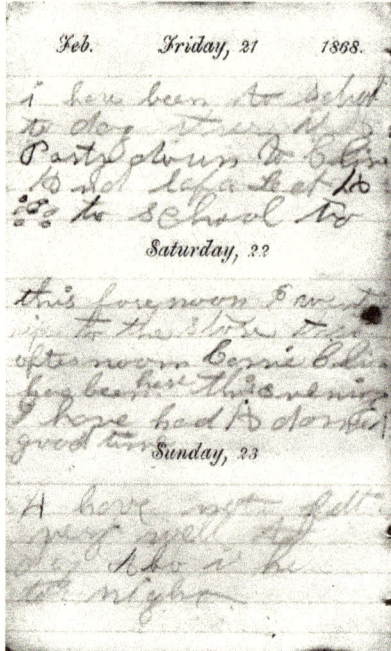

February, Monday 24, 1868
we have been to washing today but did not hang out the clothes.

February, Tuesday 25, 1868
got the work out of the way and they would not let me go to school and I cried - have been cutting out peices [pieces].

February, Wednesday 26, 1868
i went to school today. this evening i went to Jonathan's and had a darned good time.

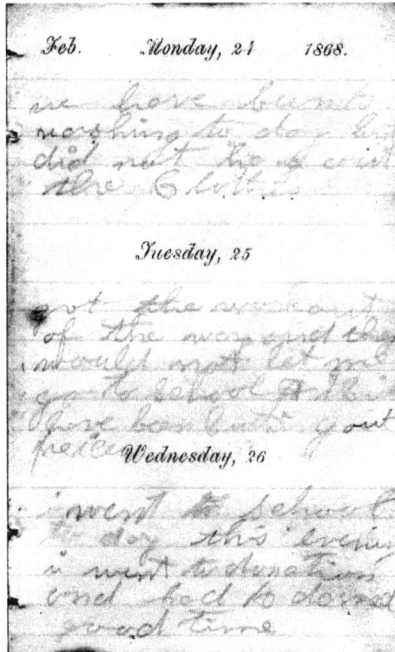

February, Thursday 27, 1868
have been to school today. it is out for good today. Velma is here - I had a Strawberry give [to] me.

February, Friday 28, 1868
Sarah and Jane went up to Pitcher today & George went down to Willett after Jane.

February, Saturday 29, 1868
i have been making my dress today. Jerome is gone up to the corners.

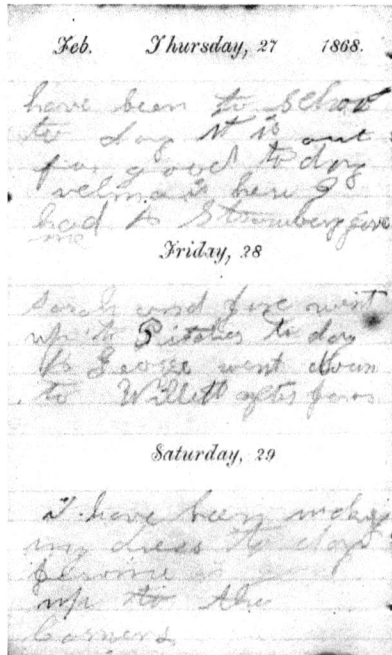

March, Sunday 1, 1868
went to Church this forenoon and the Evening i did not go - Abb is here tonight.

March, Monday 2, 1868
it is blowing and storming like Everything. we did not wash today. Hoag and Bill Andrews is here.

March, Tuesday 3, 1868
we have been to washing today and it is so we can get to the Corners.

March, Wednesday 4, 1868

today is my birthday and i went up to Pa's a little while and it is quite pleasant today.

March, Thurday 5, 1868

I went up to Pitcher [New York] today. This afternoon Mrs. ----'s folks is here and staid the Evening - And Abb was here.

March, Friday 6, 1868

We Churned today - did not go eny where today.

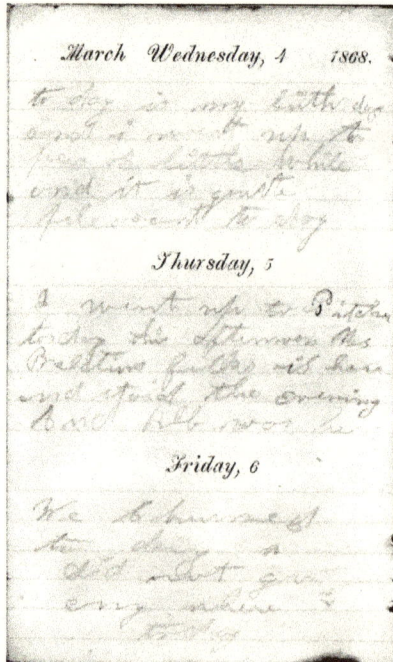

March, Saturday 7, 1868
the girls went up to the Store and Post Office. I heard from Velma and she was sewing on Herb's shirt.

March, Sunday 8, 1868
Carrie stops in here this forenoon but i did not go to Church - went this Evening. Dr. Greene is buried today.

March, Monday 9, 1868
we have been a-washing today - did not go to the post office this afternoon - Jane and Abb went to Cincinnatus.

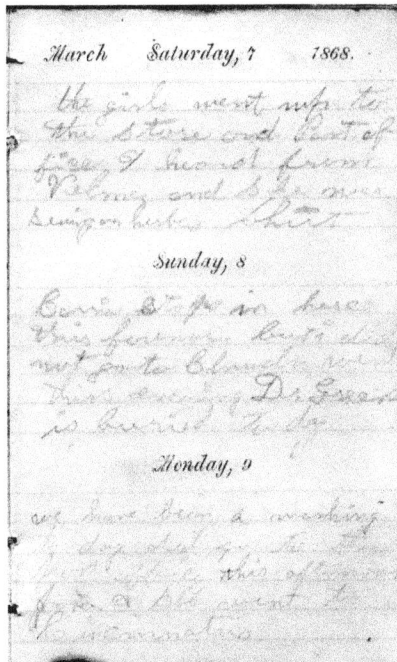

March, Tuesday 10, 1868
have been to work today - did not step out eny where today.

March, Wednesday 11, 1868
Jane and I went up to the post office and I see Frank & Carrie. Lafa come home with me.

March, Thursday 12, 1868
Lafa Staid all night and was down early. Jane and Sarah went to Whitney today. Lib S---- is here.

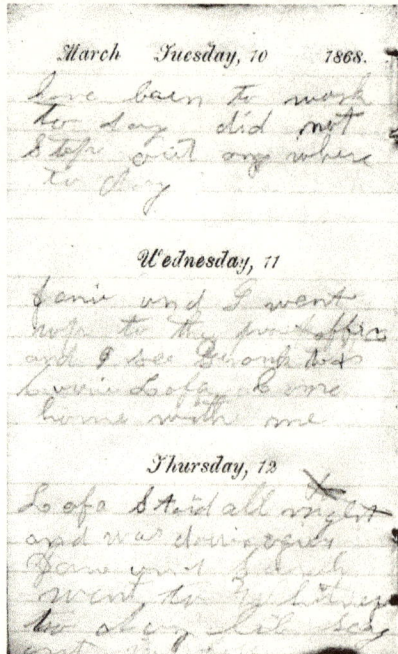

March, Friday 13, 1868
George and Uncle Noel went after Jerome. Anna and Mercell was here this afternoon.

March, Saturday 14, 1868
I have been making pies today. Uncle Willie is going to have Donations. Aunt Harriet was here.

March, Sunday 15, 1868
i went to Church today - come home did not go tonight ------. Abb is here.

March, Monday 16, 1868
did the washing this forenoon and this afternoon went to Mrs.
Holmes funrel - there was a good many there. Roselle and George
brought the syrup down and we had some molasses for supper.

March, Tuesday 17, 1868
Dayton Shufelt come and brought some Apples - have not heard
from Velma today - but spose she is getting along as well as pos-
sible.

March, Wednesday 18, 1868
have been up to the Store twice today and went to Donation to
----- but did not have so good a time as did to Osborn's Donations. come home about 5 after 12.

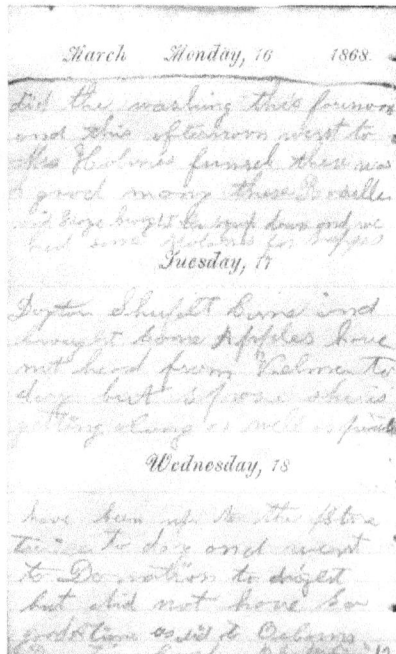

March, Thursday 19, 1868
the girls went to Mrs. Ganner [Tanner?] this afternoon and Carrie Cline come along and we went to post office and had a good time but did not get much of enything.

March, Friday 20, 1868
have been a-sewing today. Sophia come down and braided Jane's hair. we went over to uncle John's and got the h------. Em Bennett has tried to have a baby.

March, Saturday 21, 1868
it has been snowing today like the Devil all day long. have not heard from Velma today spose she'll get along without me. have been sewing.

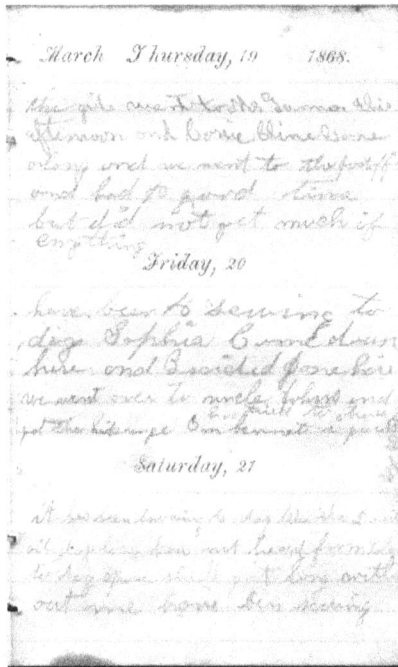

March, Sunday 22, 1868
went to Church this forenoon. Carrie come along and went.
evening have got company.

March, Monday 23, 1868
have been to washing today and I am very tired. there came
a peddler to our house and he wanted to stay all night so we
let him.

March, Tuesday 24, 1868
this Morning i had a present give to me. went to uncle Nelson
and Rose came home with me to stay all night.

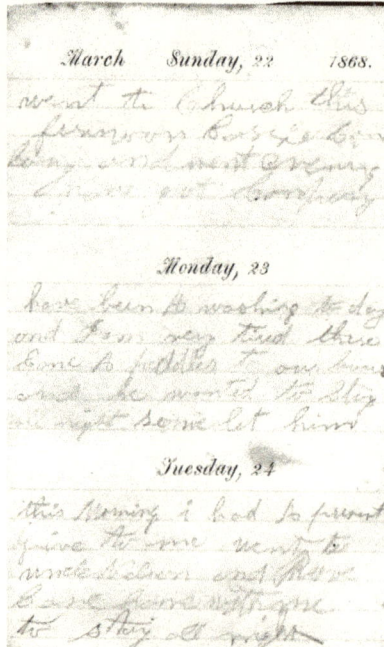

March, Wednesday 25, 1868

we have been a-sugaring off today. i went to the post office
and Lafa come down to stay all night.

March, Thursday 26, 1868

the Girls went up to Pa's to see uncle Willie. Mrs. Ganner
[Tanner?] and Manerva has been here. We sugared off. Herb
has come down to stay all night.

March, Friday 27, 1868

i went up to Mr. Jones's and this afternoon Carrie Cline came
over a-visiting. Oscar and his wife and Velma is here a-going
to stay all night. sugared off tonight.

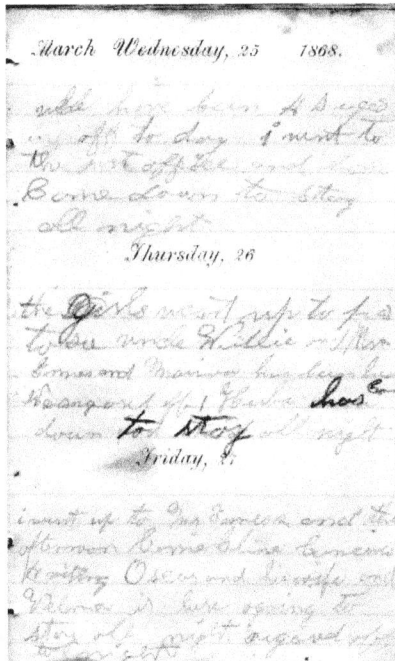

March, Saturday 28, 1868
we have sugared off 2 today. Almira Potter died yesterday and is buried tomorrow about 1 o'clock.

March, Sunday 29, 1868
I went to Church is forenoon and after I came back went up to the sugar bush. Wrote a letter and went to meeting this evening. Abb is here.

March, Monday 30, 1868
We have been to washing today. Sugared off 2 today.

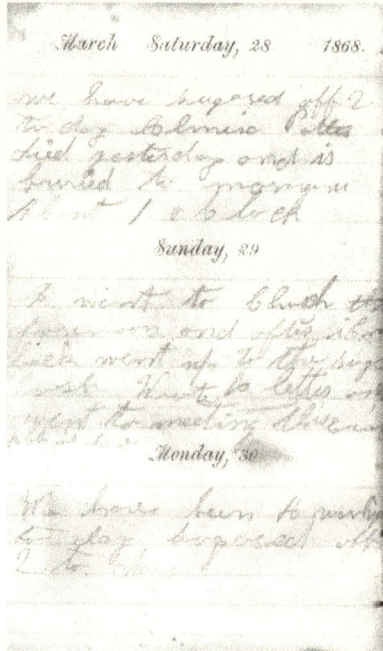

March, Tuesday 31, 1868
Went to the store and went to Mr. Cline's to stay all night.

April, Wednesday 1, 1868
Staid all night to Mr. Cline's. had got fooled 2 [twice] today. have not heard from Velma today but spose she will.

April, Thursday 2, 1868
the grafting men has been here today most all day. we emptied our feather beds today. Aunt Betsy has been here.

April, Friday 3, 1868
I have been up to Pa's to get Velma's dress patterns. Mr. Osborns girls have been here and Sophia and Mrs. West to [too].

April, Saturday 4, 1868
[No entry]

April, Sunday 5, 1868
I went to Church today and this evening. we had company - Mr. Abb Clark.

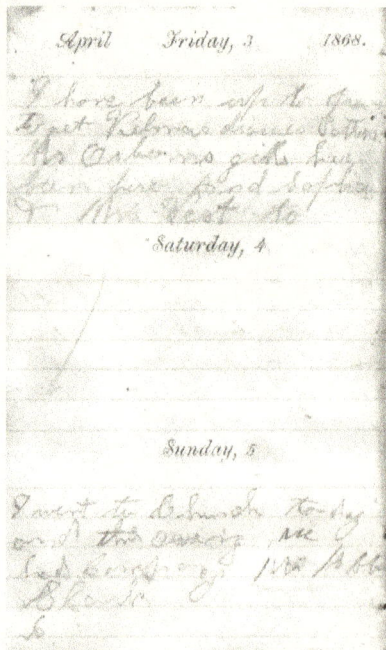

April, Monday 6, 1868
we have been a-washing today. got the washing out of the way and the girls went to Examinations and staid till night.

April, Tuesday 7, 1868
It has been Snowing like Everything. Snowed all day long and i have been to sewing today most all the time.

April, Wednesday 8, 1868
We have had Company today. Mr. Wentworth and his wife.

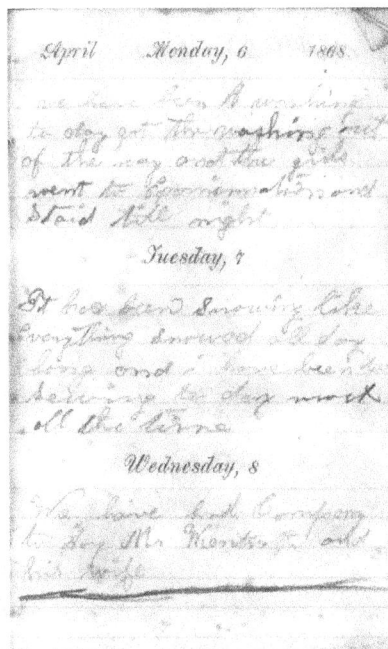

April, Thursday 9, 1868
has been snowing all day. it is real ------. I cut my fingers tonight and Jane went to go back [and] she fell down.

April, Friday 10, 1868
the girls and Jerome has gone up to uncle Amos' today. it has
been snowing. i went up to the [post] office and Velma came
down.

April, Saturday 11, 1868
Velma staid all night. the girls got back about 10. Mr. Ellis
and his wife has been to ----- -----. I guess that Abb is not going into the Store.

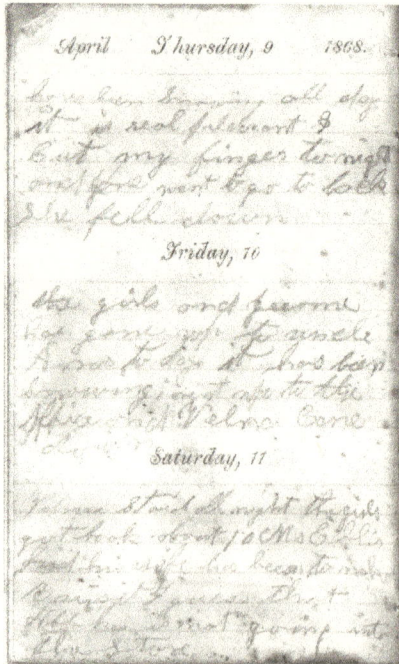

April, Sunday 12, 1868
i went to Church today and this Evening. Mr. Woodard preached to [too].

April, Monday 13, 1868
we have been to washing today.

April, Tuesday 14, 1868
we done most all of our ironing today. Jane and Sophia went to Mr. Clark's this afternoon. It rained.

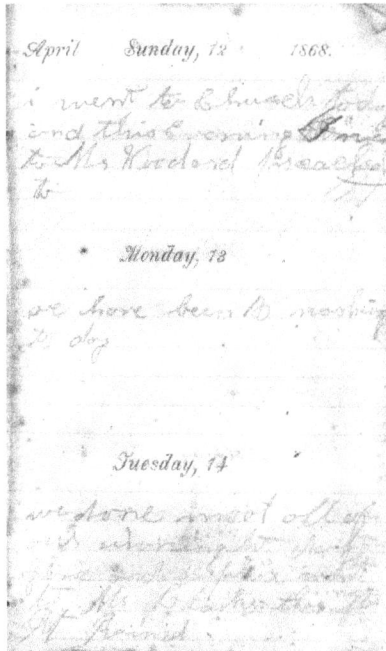

April, Wednesday 15, 1868
it is Raining today.

April, Thursday 16, 1868
it has been raining some today.

April , Friday 17, 1868
It has been raining today. Inez West has been here a-visiting. i
went to the tanners today.

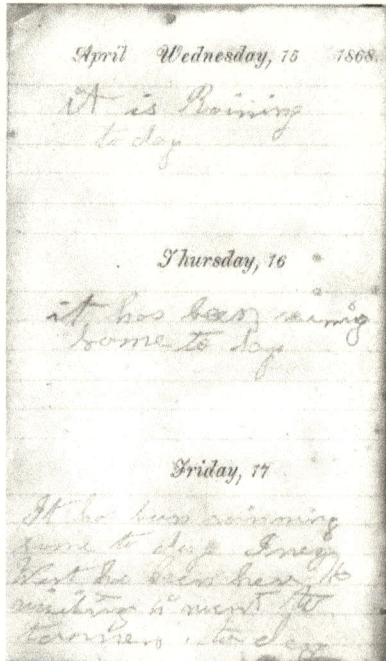

April, Saturday 18, 1868
we have sugared off to day. I have not been doing much of enything today.

April, Sunday 19, 1868
it is real pleasant today. I went out to Uncle Philander's. Vel and I got Lafa - she is not very Well. went to meeting this Evening.

April, Monday 20, 1868
we have been a-washing today but did not yet hang out Clothes.

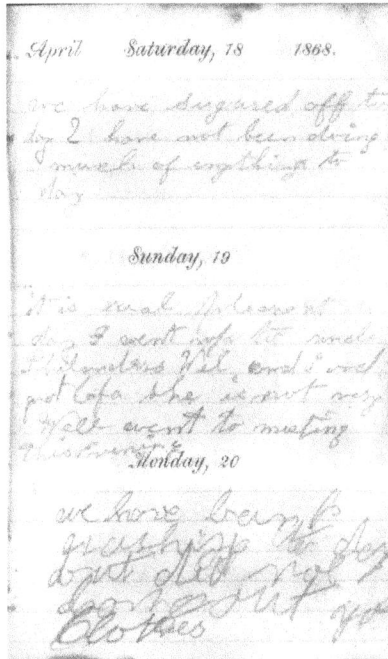

April, Tuesday 21, 1868
Aunt Lucy and i went up to Mr. harrison's this afternoon. Orion is up.

April, Wednesday 22, 1868
we hung out our Clothes today. Hut is here tonight and so is Evie.

April, Thursday 23, 1868
have been over to uncle John's today twice. Velma and i went and got some birch. Carrie is here.

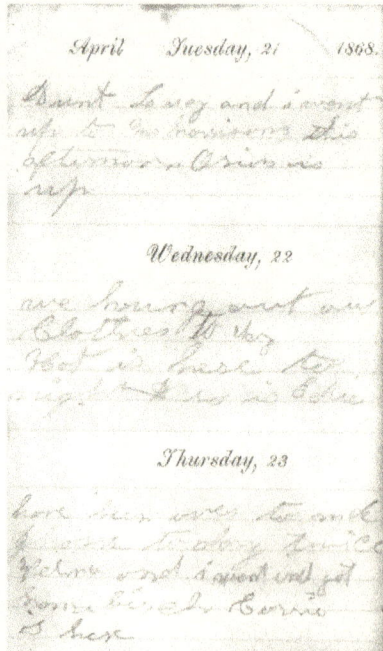

April, Friday 24, 1868
Carrie staid here last night and we had lots of fun. i went up and got 2 quarts of oil, box of Matches today.

April, Saturday 25, 1868
i have got a hard Cold today - have not done much today.

April, Sunday 26, 1868
did not go to Church today.

April, Monday 27, 1868
We did our washing and tonight my throat is sore.

April, Tuesday 28, 1868
we have been making soap today. Uncle Willie is worse.

April, Wednesday 29, 1868
have heard from Uncle Willie - he hain't any better.

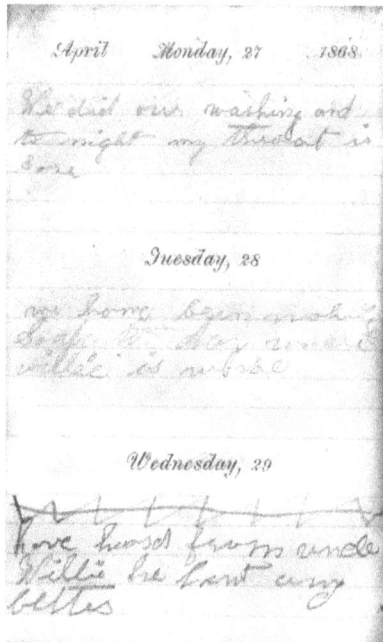

April, Thursday 30, 1868
Uncle Willie is worse today.

May, Friday, 1, 1868
Uncle Willie died about 7 this morning. Jane went up there this afternoon.

May, Saturday 2, 1868
I have been up to see Uncle Willie. Lafa came home with me.

May, Sunday 3, 1868
Lafa come down again this afternoon. Jane and Jerome went to funrel and Velma and Minnie came down today.

May, Monday 4, 1868
we have been washing today - washed a good many things.

May, Tuesday 5, 1868
we have been Cleaning house today all day. George got some fish - Cleaned them.

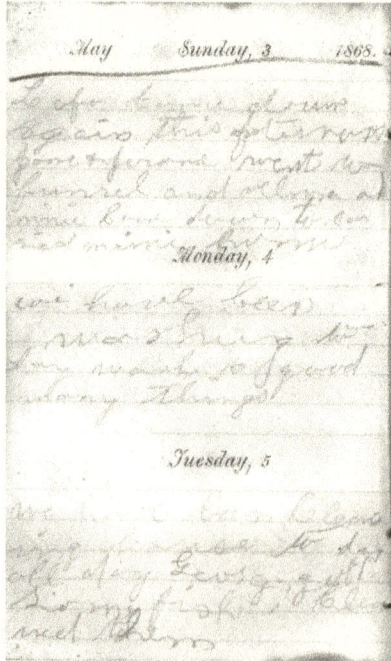

May, Wednesday 6, 1868
Albert Ellis and Alsha Potter is married. Oscar & his wife and
Ed Knapp and Helen are here. Sophia come down and said
that Ed had his arm around Helen when they went by.

May, Thursday 7, 1868
it has been raining most all day. i went up and got the paper
of --- - we put down the carpet today.

May, Friday 8, 1868
we have been cleaning the milkroom today. i went to the post
office today. hulda is not feeling quite well today.

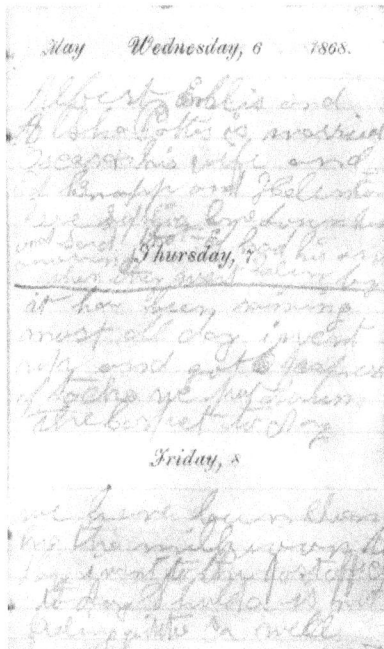

May, Saturday 9, 1868
Rose and Dora has been making a Visit. Jerome is going to give me 50 cts.

May, Sunday 10, 1868
went to meeting this Evening. hurt my knee today.

May, Monday 11, 1868
uncle Noel and Jerome went to Cortland. Aunt Lucy & Jane & Sarah went to Aunt Harriet's.

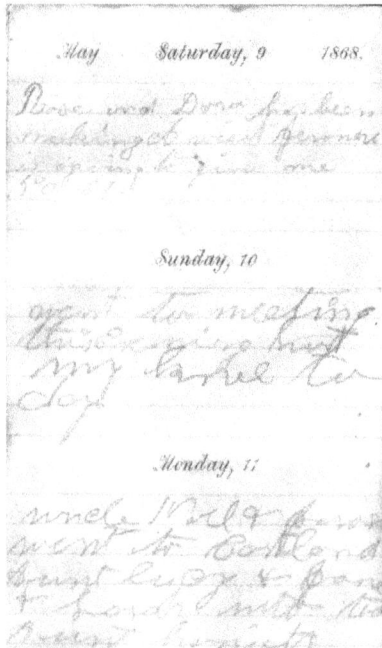

May, Tuesday 12, 1868
[no entry]

May, Wednesday 13, 1868
work in the dooryard today.

May, Thursday 14, 1868
we Cleaned the kitchen today. Mary came down.

May, Friday 15, 1868
we worked in the dooryard. I am real tired.

May, Saturday 16, 1868
i went up to Aunt Harriet's a-visiting today.

May, Sunday 17, 1868
went to Church today. it rained today.

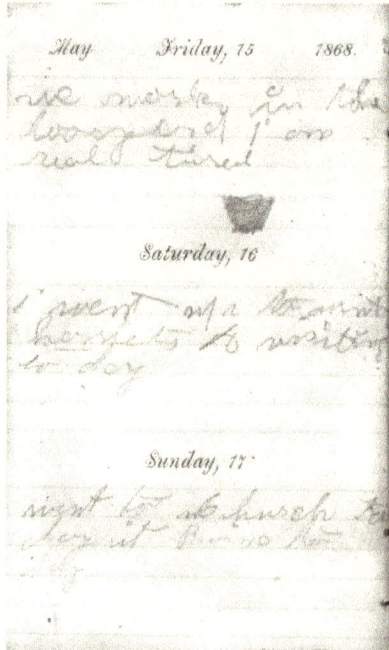

May, Monday 18, 1868
we have been washing today. it rains.

May, Tuesday 19, 1868
it raines today. Jerome went to Willett tonight.

May, Wednesday 20, 1868
it rains today. Aunt Lucy and Jane went to Cincinnatus to-day.

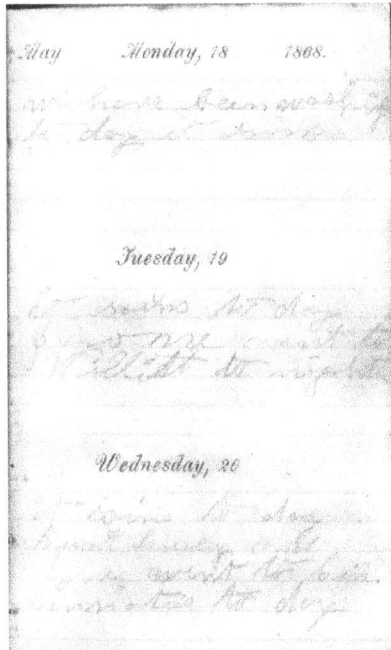

May, Thursday 21, 1868
it has rained all day today.

May, Friday 22, 1868
Aunt Lucy has gone up to Mrs. Neal's today. the girls went to
uncle Edwin's a little While.

May, Saturday 23, 1868
the girls and Aunt Lucy went to George's today.

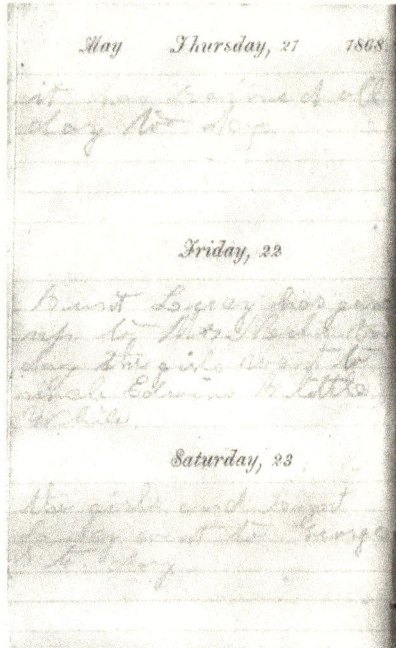

May, Sunday 24, 1868
went to Church today and tonight.

May, Monday 25, 1868
we have been to a-washing today and to black the stove. it is not very pleasant.

May, Tuesday 26, 1868
Lafa Staid here last night. Velma, Carrie, & i went and got the -------. Velma is here.

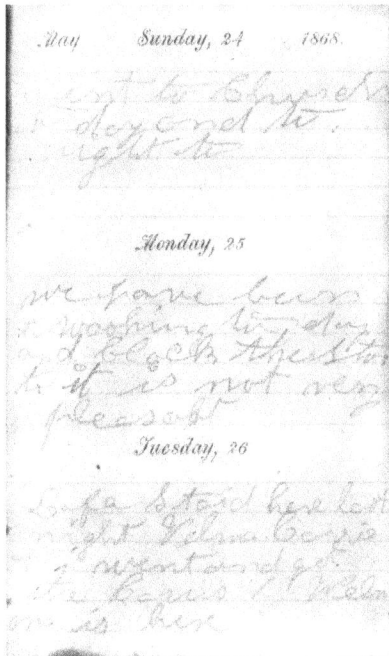

May, Wednesday 27, 1868
Velma Staid all night last night. i went to school for the first day. dewit has been here.

May, Thursday 28, 1868
i went to school today. i like the teacher - first rate.

May, Friday 29, 1868
we Cleaned the schoolhouse today. Mrs. Clark and the Baby, Miss Collins.

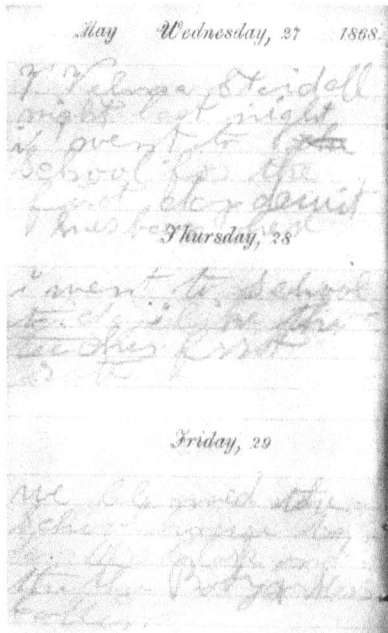

May, Saturday 30, 1868
it has not been pleasant today.

May, Sunday 31, 1868
went to meeting twice today.

June, Monday 1, 1868
we washed today - it has rained some. i went to school.

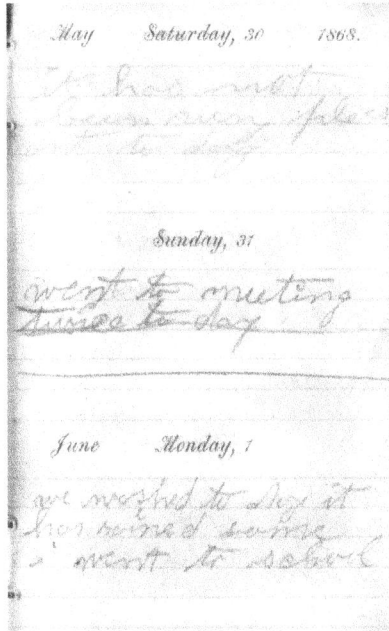

June, Tuesday 2, 1868

i went to school. Aunt hulda is here this afternoon. the girls went to Mr. Brown's.

June, Wednesday 3, 1868

went to school. Mrs. Hakes is here.

June, Thursday 4, 1868

Mrs. Hakes staid all night. Aunt Lucy and uncle Noel has gone to fabius [Fabius, New York]. Jane gone to Whitney.

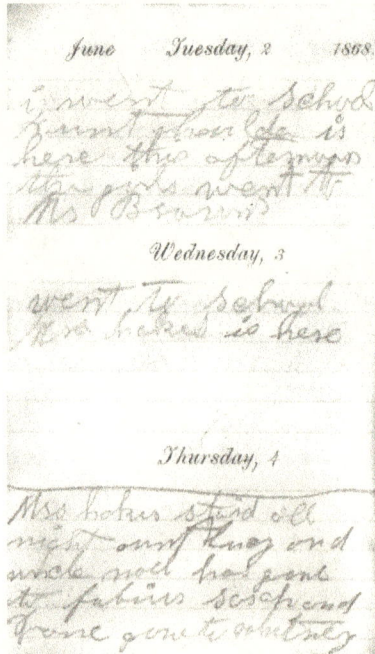

June, Friday 5, 1868
Carrie and Velma staid all night last night. the girls went to Mrs. Rathbone's last Evening.

June, Saturday 6, 1868
it has been raining all day most. i went up to Pa's this afternoon.

June, Sunday 7, 1868
went to Church today. Aunt Lucy and uncle noel got back today.

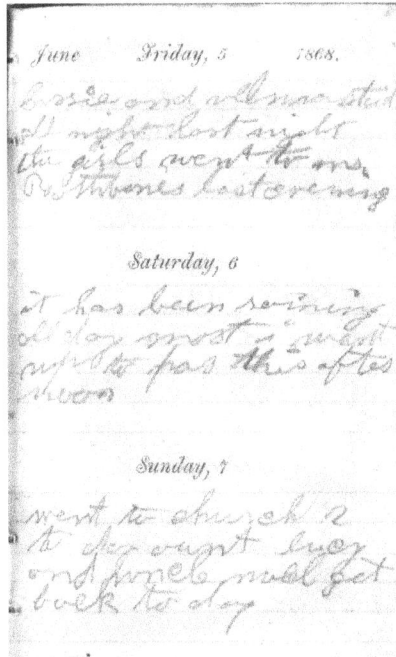

June, Monday 8, 1868
we washed today. i went to school today. i went up on the wintergreen [Wintergreen Hill]. Amelia and Velma went too.

June, Tuesday 9, 1868
the girls and Jerome has gone to Cortland a-visiting. i went to school today. the teacher staid all night last night.

June, Wednesday 10, 1868
i got around with the work and went to school.

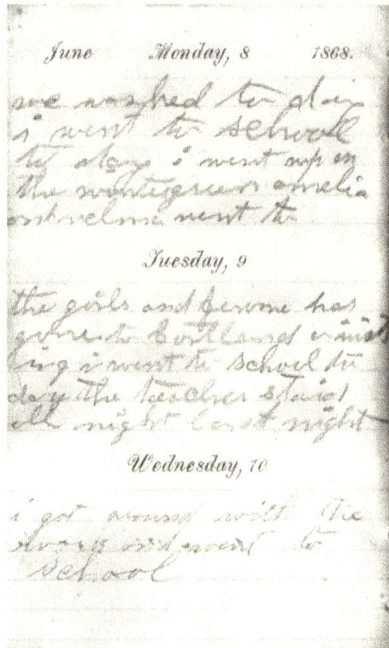

June, Thursday 11, 1868
i got around with the work and went to school. they have got back. it rained today.

June, Friday 12, 1868
i went to school today. it is pleasant.

June, Saturday 13, 1868
have been sewing today. went and rode.

June, Sunday 14, 1868
did not go to meeting today but went this Evening. Mary Hutchinson was there to [too]. Rose, Lafa, and Carrie was up here today.

June, Monday 15, 1868
we have been to working today. I went to school today - had a first-rate time. It has been a-raining a good deal.

June, Tuesday 16, 1868
I went to school today and had a first-rate time. Found 2 four-leaf clovers today. I went up to Pa's tonight.

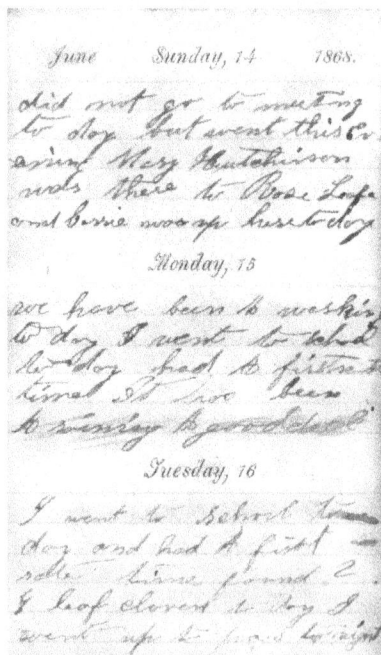

June, Wednesday 17, 1868

 I staid all night last to Pa's. went to Cincinnatus today. did
not go to school today. have been making soap.

June, Thursday 18, 1868

~~did not go to school today. helped Clean the meeting house~~
~~and is very tired. Mr. and Mrs. Wise eat dinner here.~~

June, Friday 19, 1868

~~helped clean the meeting house today and is very tired. Mr.~~
~~and Mrs. Wise eat dinner here.~~

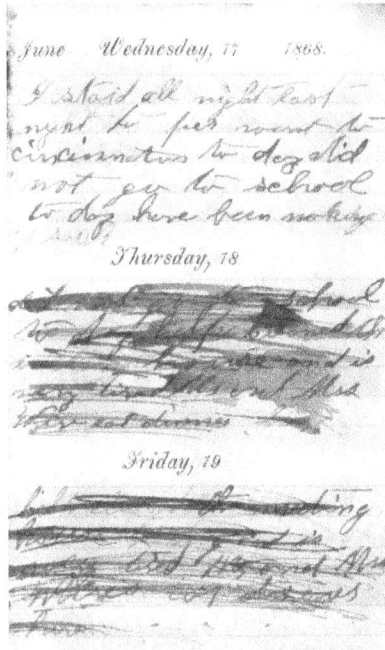

June, Saturday 20, 1868

I made the floor and helped get the work out of the way. Jane made my Sack. Uncle Noel and Aunt Lucy is a-going up to Uncle Amos'.

June, Sunday 21, 1868

I went to meeting In the forenoon and evening. 2 drovers here to stay all night. I went over to Uncle John's last night. Vel, Lafa, and I drove the cows away.

June, Monday 22, 1868

~~I kissed Abb tonight. Abb-------George ------on the----me.~~ we did not wash today. It has rained some. they bought A cow.

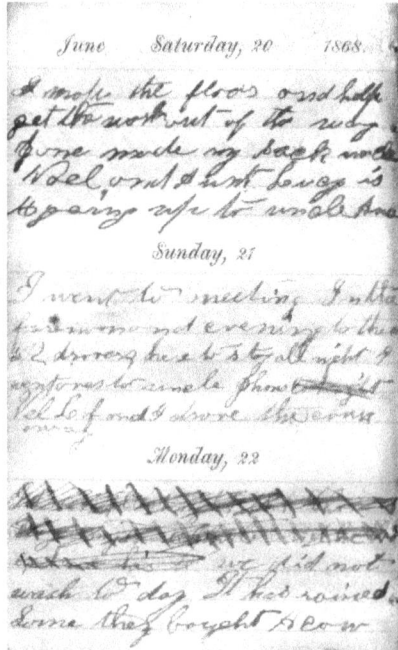

June, Tuesday 23, 1868

we have been a-washing today. the cow that they bought has
got a calf. I have been to sewing some today.

June, Wednesday 24, 1868

don't know what I have been doing to day. went to the [cheese]
factory with the milk tonight.

June, Thursday 25, 1868

Pa made me a present of a hat. Aunt Dorcas, Aunt Leib, Aunt
Betsy, Milo Clark, Sarah and the baby, Mrs. Chatfield and
Mrs. Smith.

June, Friday 26, 1868
had a present of a hat yesterday. can't write much of enything today.

June, Saturday 27, 1868
~~have been to meeting twice today . there was a girl baptized today. some one ------ with me and come home with me to-night.~~

June, Sunday 28, 1868
to meetings I went to today. has been a woman baptized today. Abb and i lock arms as we was coming home from meeting.

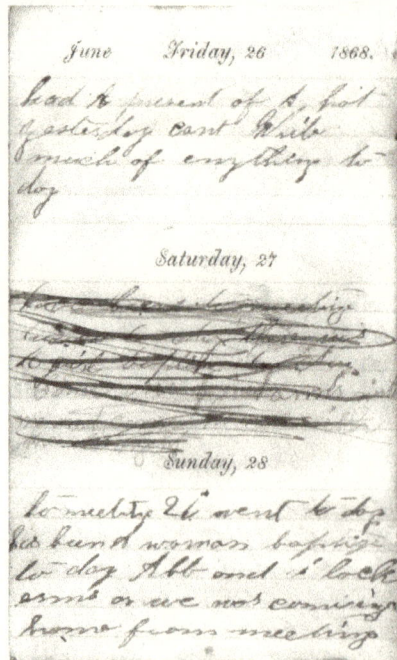

June, Monday 29, 1868

We have been a-washing today. Sarah and i went up to the store and got a ---- and some buttons.

June, Tuesday 30, 1868

Jaleana, Nancy, and Aunt Harriet have been here a-visiting today. did not go to school today.

J **uly, Wednesday 1, 1868**

I went to school to day. Ellen Pendleton is here. Amelia, Inez, and I have been up to Mrs. Wrechkels [Rockwell] to sewing.

July, Thursday 2, 1868
I staid to Mr. Osborn's last night. went to Sophia's between 10 and 11. Ell [Ellen] went today. Aunt Lucy is up to Mrs. Whitney's.

July, Friday 3, 1868
Staid to Mrs. Chatfield's last night.

July, Saturday 4, 1868
Josephine Gilmore and her husband, Velma and Mary Hutchinson has been here today. Jane, Abb, and Jerome has gone to picnic.

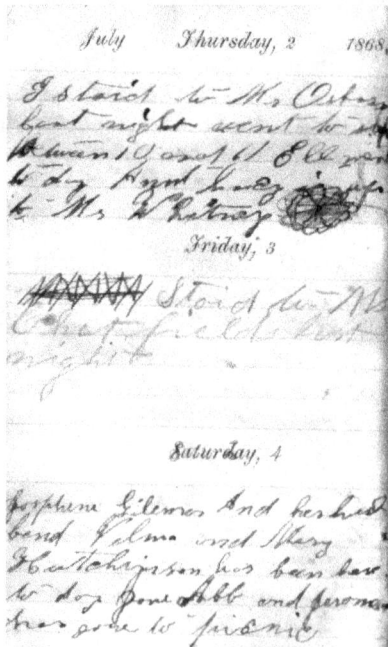

July, Sunday 5, 1868
i went to meeting to day. Velma and I went up on the Wintergreen Hill today. Abb is here tonight.

July, Monday 6, 1868
We have been a-washing. had company to school. has been somebody here too. the girls has gone up to the store.

July, Tuesday 7, 1868
Abb ----. it has rained real hard today. have been to school today. Aunt Lucy, the girls is up to Mrs. Clark's. Rozel is here.

July, Wednesday 8, 1868
It has been very pleasant. went with Velma to turn away cows. Carrie introduced me to the Silvernail girls. teacher is here tonight.

July, Thursday 9, 1868
Miss Holeroid[?] staid here all night last night. frank neal has been here today to work. it is a very beautiful day today.

July, Friday 10, 1868
we spoke pieces today but did not go off very well. Aunt Lucy, Sarah, and Jane is over to Uncle John's.

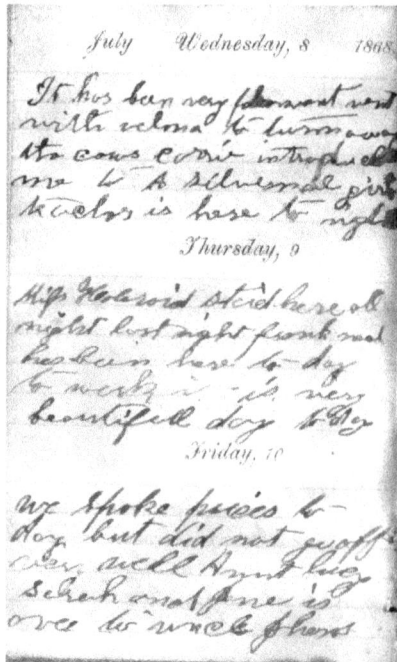

July, Saturday 11, 1868
[No entry]

July, Sunday 12, 1868
have been to meeting 2 day. I saw Mate there. Oscar has been and so has Aunt Dorc, Uncle John, and Uncle Chauncey. Abb is here.

July, Monday 13, 1868
we have been a-washing. I did not go to School today but went to the post office. I seen a man and woman go in a-swimming.

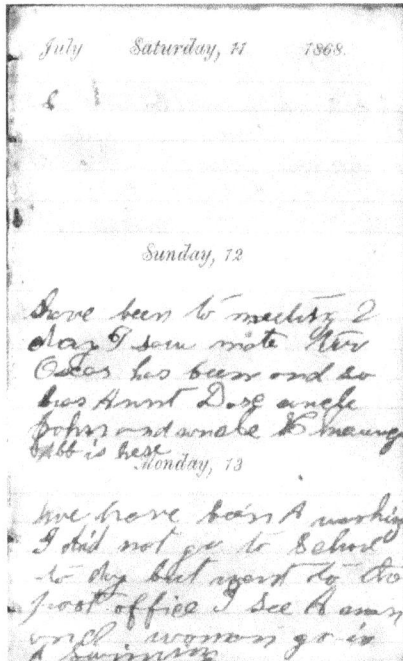

July, Tuesday 14, 1868
went up to Mr. Hutchinson's tonight. had some cherries. went to school today. I seen Abb tonight. it is real hot.

July, Wednesday 15, 1868
Staid all night - had a good time. been to school today. It is hotter than the Devil.

July, Thursday 16, 1868
Ma [stepmother] and the teacher is here tonight. it is a little cooler.

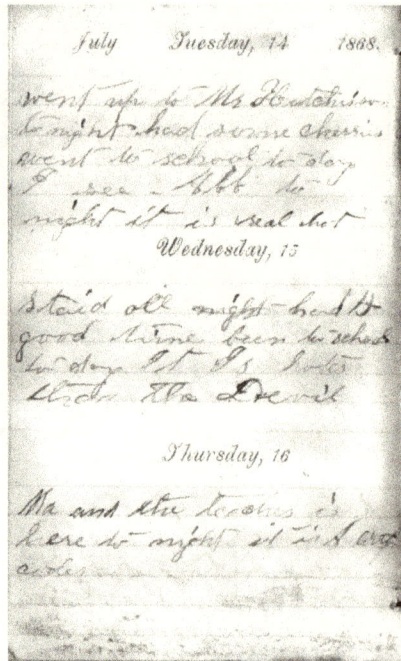

July, Friday 17, 1868
The teacher is here today. noon Frank finished work today.

July, Saturday 18, 1868
Denton, Grover, Herbert, George, Lafa, Velma and Rozelle and i went a-berrying - did not get many.

July, Sunday 19, 1868
Abb and Jane come home from meeting ----- and went in to ------. Abb -------finished the ----- had a real good time.

July, Monday 20, 1868
been a-washing. Emmes Sergeant and Lib has been here. did not go to School today. went up to Pa's, uncle Nelson's, uncle Edwin's, and Mr. Neal's.

July, Tuesday 21, 1868
the girls went up to Nick Cyrus. I went to school. Minnie Monroe come home with me. Mrs. Rogers is here.

July, Wednesday 22, 1868
Velma, Rosa, and i went a-berrying today & got 6 quarts - quite tired tonight. Aunt Dorc is here.

July, Thursday 23. 1868
I went to school today - it has rained like everything. Dent come home with me. got soking wet. Aunt Dorc is here.

July, Friday 24, 1868
i went to school today - had lots of fun.

July, Saturday 25, 1868
[No entry]

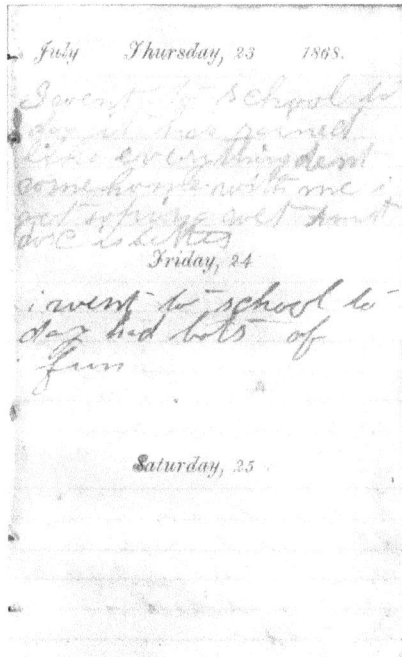

July, Sunday 26, 1868
have been to Church twice today. Inez & Lafa has been here today. Abb is here tonight. I saw Mate tonight.

July, Monday 27, 1868
we have been washing today, Sarah is over to uncle John's to work. went to school this afternoon.

July, Tuesday 28, 1868
have been at school today. Aunt Lucy is gone up to Mrs. Loomis.

July, Wednesday 29, 1868
I have been to Mrs. Clines today a-visiting. Lizzie Wrockwell [Rockwell] has been to see me but i was not at home.

July, Thursday 30, 1868
Mrs. Chatfield, Mrs. Cline, --- Delet, and her baby is here and Mrs. Fish. I have come down to Uncle John's to commence work tomorrow.

July, Friday 31, 1868
got up this morning. did not do much but the work today.

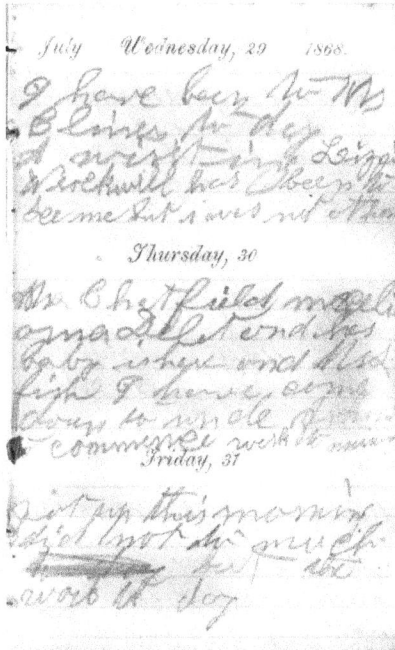

August, Saturday 1, 1868

have been a-baking today. tonight I went home. Velma and Hut was there.

August, Sunday 2, 1868

have been at Church 2 today. Abb is here tonight. I did not go in to see him.

August, Monday 3, 1868

Aunt Dorc and i did the washing today. very tired tonight.

August, Tuesday 4, 1868
baked this forenoon. this afternoon picked wool. Aunt Lucy has been over and brought my finished dress. did not stay long.

August, Wednesday 5, 1868
I got the work out of the way and Churned and this afternoon have been picking wool I am over home to stay all night.

August, Thursday 6, 1868
I Ironed and wash 2 shirts. Uncle John & Pa has gone to Cortland. have been picking wool. It has rained today.

August, Friday 7, 1868
Jerome came over and brought me a pair of stockings. have been picking wool ever since Delett and Edith has been here.

August, Saturday 8, 1868
I went up and had my feet measured. finished picking the wool. Barton's folks is here. I see Velma today. the baby is pretty.

August, Sunday 9, 1868
have been at meeting 2 today. went up to the [cheese] factory. Abb is here. i see Mate tonight. Abb has been here before today.

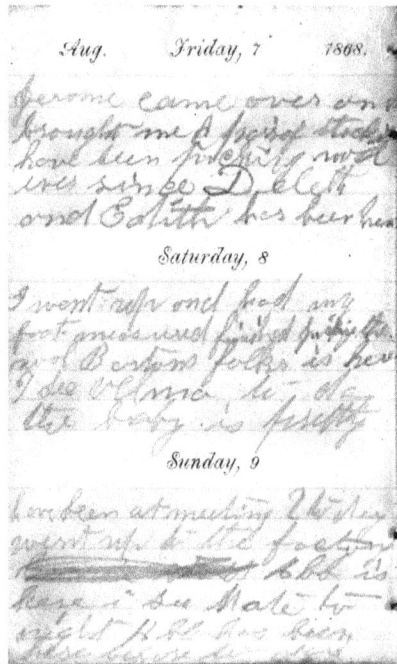

August, Monday 10, 1868
have washed, mopped, ironed, baked today. have come over home to stay all night. Julius is here tonight.

August, Tuesday 11, 1868
Come over home tonight. Aunt Lucy is sick. Jerome and Bart went with the cheese. It has rained quite hard today.

August, Wednesday 12, 1868
Aunt Betsy, Sarah, and Bart and his wife and Children is here. gone up to the store this afternoon. I went up and got me a thimble.

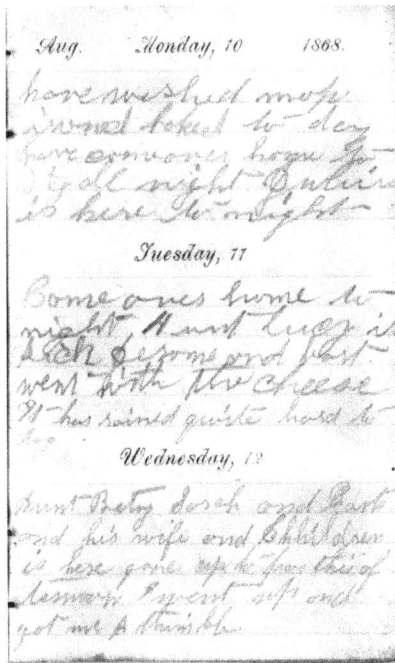

August, Thursday 13, 1868
Sarah and Aunt Lucy, Aunt Betsy and Bart and his wife and
children has been down with Lunise a-visiting. i see Lina tonight. Sarah is sick.

August, Friday 14, 1868
baked bread today. Aunt Dorc went over to the store. Lu-
nice & Amelia and Mrs. Cline has been here today. had my
thimble ma--.

August, Saturday 15, 1868
have been a-sewing today. Minor and Frank is down to stay all
night. Aunt Dorc and I went over in the swamp tonight.

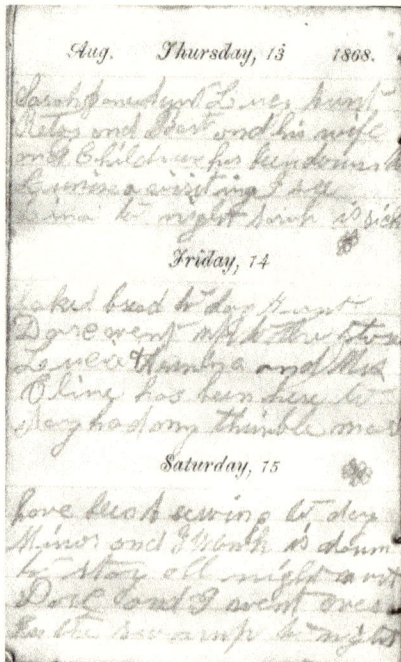

August, Sunday 16, 1868
Did not go to Church today but went this evening. Abb
Come home with Jane tonight. Mate gave me an apple. Abb
Is here tonight.

August, Monday 17, 1868
we washed today. went over home tonight. Aunt Lucy has
gone up to Lu Sargent, and the girls and Abb and Jerome has
gone to the Locks.

August, Tuesday 18, 1868
The Teacher Is here tonight. have not done much today. Aunt
Dorc has gone up to stay to uncle Edwin's this afternoon and
left me to bake the bread.

August, Wednesday 19, 1868
Abb come down this forenoon and shingled my hair. It has rained reel hard today. did not go home tonight. Jerome went to Whitney Point today.

August, Thursday 20, 1868
Went over home to stay tonight. And Osphia [Sophia] come over yesterday. they did not like it because i had my hair shingled.

August, Friday 21, 1868
Went to School this afternoon. had a first rate good time. School is out today. Got a card. did not go home tonight.

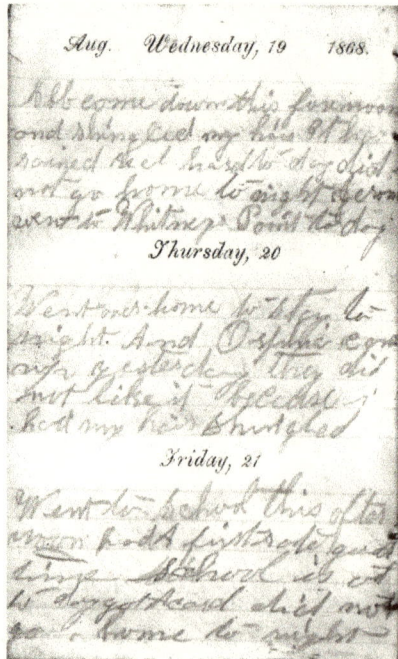

August, Saturday 22, 1868
Aunt Dorc went up to uncle Edwin's and left me to bake the bread. i See Abb a-riding out with Mary. He look neat.

August, Sunday 23, 1868
went to Church twice today. Abb come down here and eat supper. had a rooster. Abb is here again tonight.

August, Monday 24, 1868
had a very large washing today. went up to Mr. Clark's and got some papers that Abb had. I might take the girls. Osphia [Sophia] and Aunt Lucy has been here.

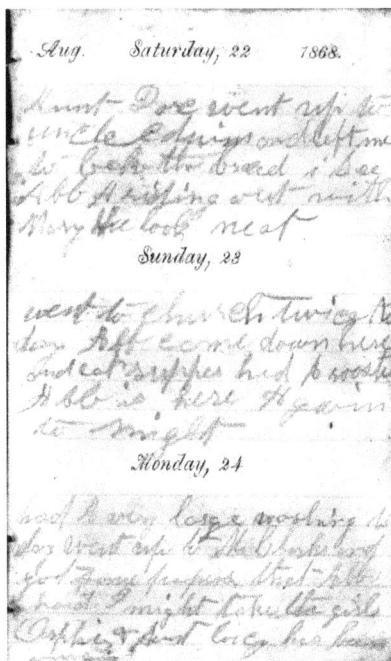

August, Tuesday 25, 1868
Oscar and his wife has been here today.

August, Wednesday 26, 1868
hurt

August, Thursday 27, 1868
[No entry]

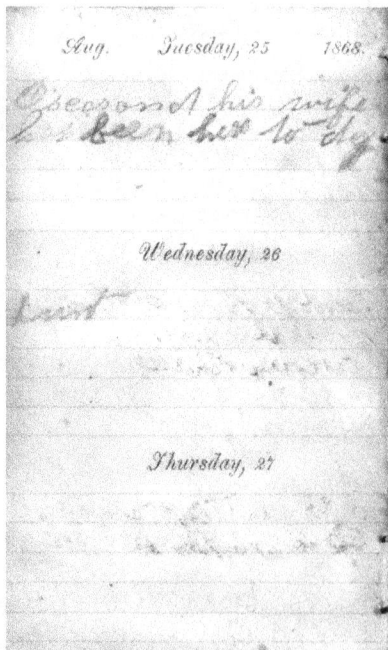

August, Friday 28, 1868
[No entry]

August, Saturday 29, 1868
been a-washing today. been very tired.

August, Sunday 30, 1868
did not go to Church today.

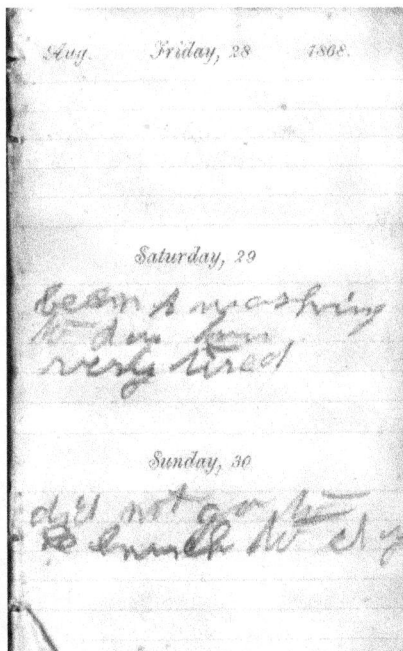

August, Monday 31, 1868
have picked one box of hops today. ~~was sick and had Abb ---~~
~~============.~~

September, Tuesday 1, 1868
picked one box of hops today and after supper for a little
while. i was taken sick and to go to the house.

September, Wednesday 2, 1868
have picked 3 boxes today. Aunt Lucy & Aunt Mary
have been here and lots of Company.

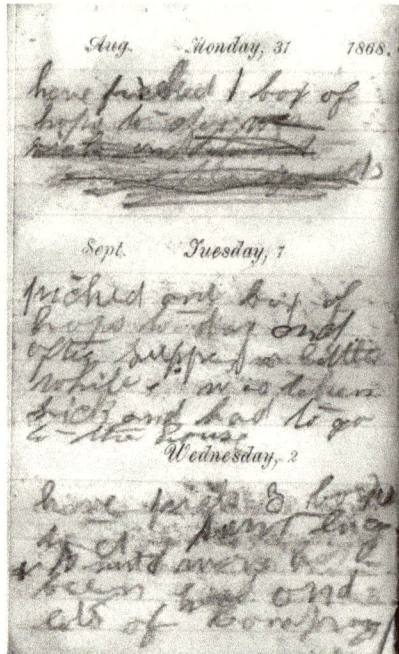

September, Thursday 3, 1868
I box and a half. had lots of friends.

September, Friday 4, 1868
pick one box and a half. It has been kinda lonesome. ---- just
got back.

September, Saturday 5, 1868
have picked 3 boxes. got through today. went home tonight.

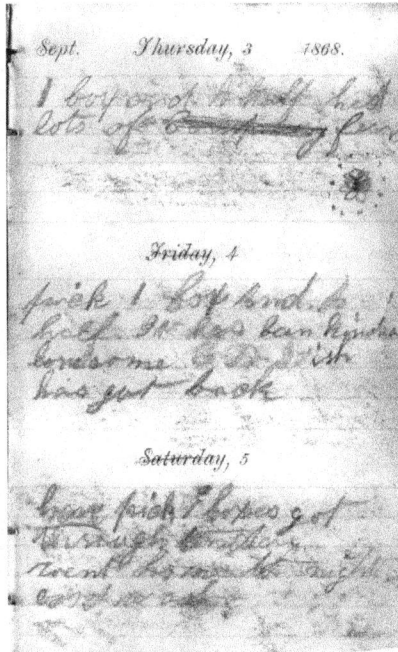

September, Sunday 6, 1868
did not go to Church today. it has been a-raining. have been Ironing today. have seen blue jays 2.

September, Monday 7, 1868
Went to Lock's to pick today. picked one box and a half.

September, Tuesday 8, 1868
have picked one box and a half. staid to Pa's last night. slept real good.

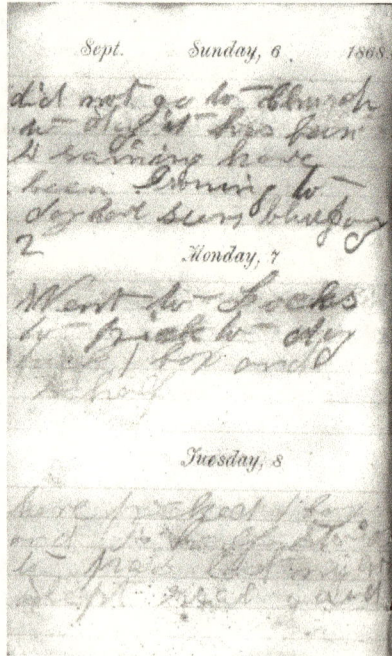

September, Wednesday 9, 1868
picked 4 and a half boxes in all. Osphia [Sophia], Jerome and George came over. It has rained quite a good ---.

September, Thursday 10, 1868
It has rained so that we did not go over to the Lock's today. have not been doing much of anything today.

September, Friday 11, 1868
It Rained So we did not go today. went to Pa's and Mr. Clark's today. had some yellow plums.

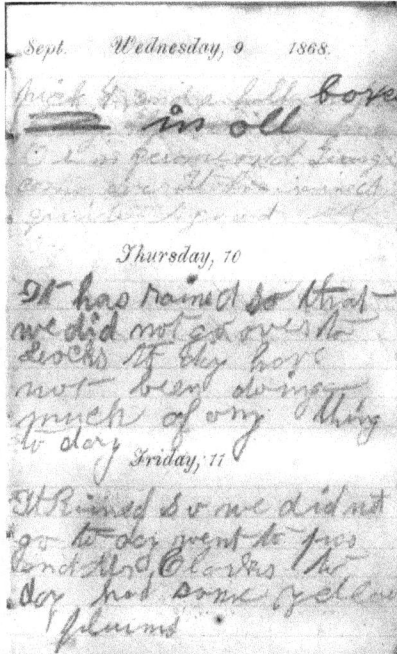

September, Saturday 12, 1868
have been picking hops today. picked 1 box. Blue Jay has been here twice today. rode over and helped out. Jerome + Osphia [Sophia] has gone to Cortland.

September, Sunday 13, 1868
went to Church 2 today. have not seen Abb - guess he hain't got back yet.

September, Monday 14, 1868
picked a half a box today.

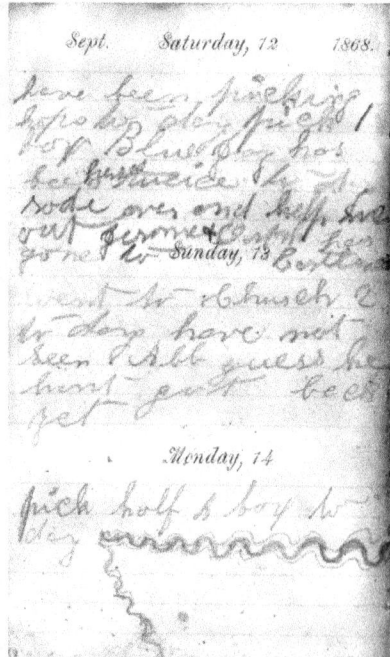

September, Tuesday 15, 1868
picked 5/8 of a box. they took up the string pieces. Abb would not let us ride. we had to walk the Stringers. Fred came home with me.

September, Wednesday 16, 1868
It has rained a good deal today. Aunt Hulda staid here last night. did not get to pick today.

September, Thursday 17, 1868
Vel and I went up to Uncle Edward's to stay all night.

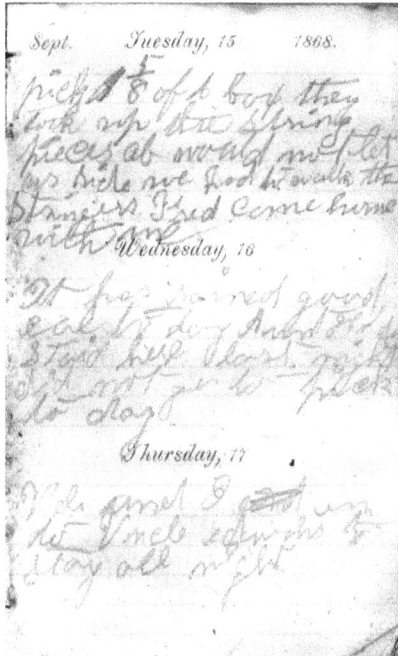

September, Friday 18, 1868
the girls went over after the pay. had cheated Sarah out of 1 box and 2/8 of a box. been to Mrs. Pritchard's a-visiting. had a good time.

September, Saturday 19, 1868
did not go any[where]. it has rained.

September, Sunday 20, 1868
Jane and I went to the post office. come round and see Abb. it has rained all day. Abb is not here.

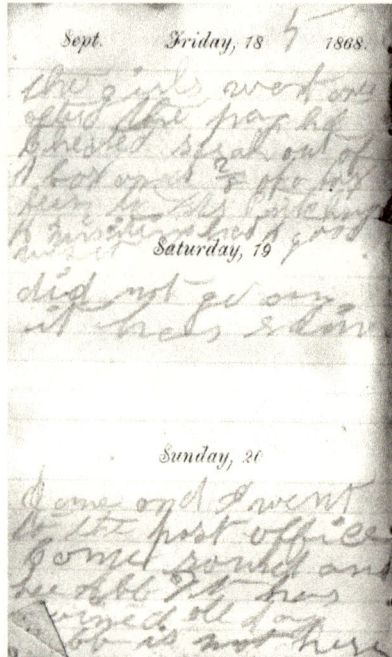

September, Monday 21, 1868
we have been a-washing today. went to the post office.

September, Tuesday 22, 1868
It has rained today.

September, Wednesday 23, 1868
It has rained a little today.

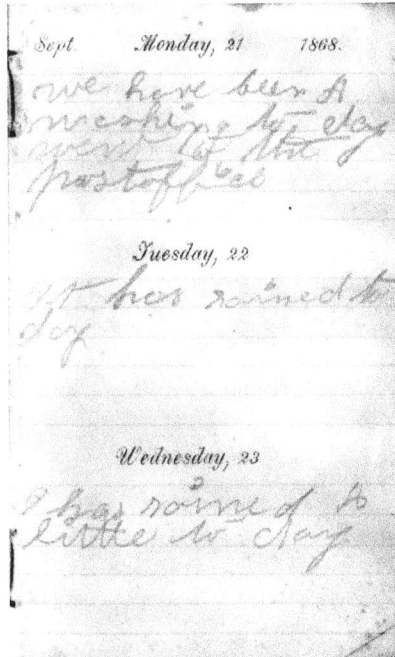

September, Thursday 24, 1868
I have been to the post office today. Aunt Dorc, Aunt Martha, Uncle Will, and Lydia has been here.

September, Friday 25, 1868
they all went away. It has rained all day long. Uncle Chancy has been here. I cried because I wanted to go up to the post office.

September, Saturday 26, 1868
went to the post office today. Lafa come down to stay all night.

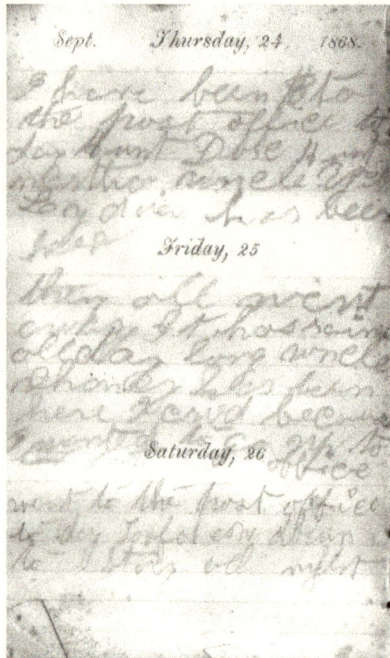

September, Sunday 27, 1868

went to Church twice today. Abb is here tonight. ~~I went in to~~
~~===. I kissed him ----- and I love him.~~

September, Monday 28, 1868

we did not wash today. Mercebia Lyons and Garret Wrockwell Is married. Jane & Abb went. Sarah has gone over to Mr.
Weaver's to work.

September, Tuesday 29, 1868

Jane began her Wreath today. I have been up to Union Valley
to meeting. see Ellen Morris & Delia Burger. have seen Abb
today.

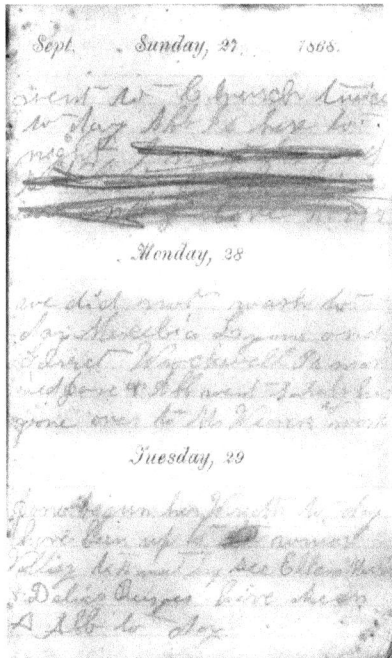

September, Wednesday 30, 1868
we washed today but the clothes look like the devil. seen Abb
& Mary.

October, **Thursday 1, 1868**
we have washed again today. Jerome fell out of a tree
today. we picked up apples to Mr. Bennett's today.
Aunt Dorc has been here today.

October, Friday 2, 1868
I have Ironed today. we paired apples tonight. Uncle Chauncey has been here.

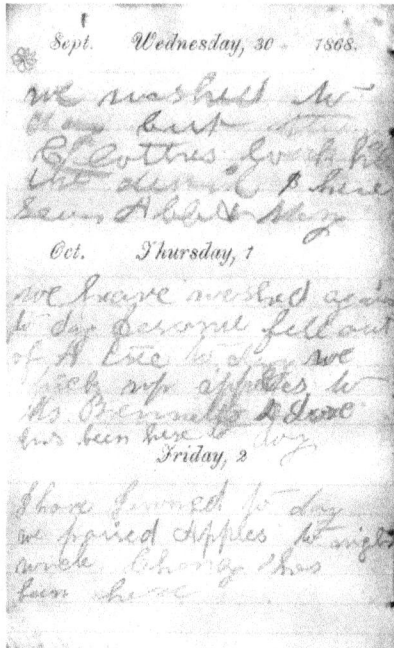

October, Saturday 3, 1868
Emmes has been here today.I went up to see Jane's wreath today. It is real pretty. I have come up to stay all night.

October, Sunday 4, 1868
I have seen Mate today. Abb is here tonite. I went in [his room] a little while. ~~Abb --- ---- ---- ---- ---- ---.~~

October, Monday 5, 1868
we did not wash today. Abb has gone to Sarah today. I have been helping Jane on wreath today.

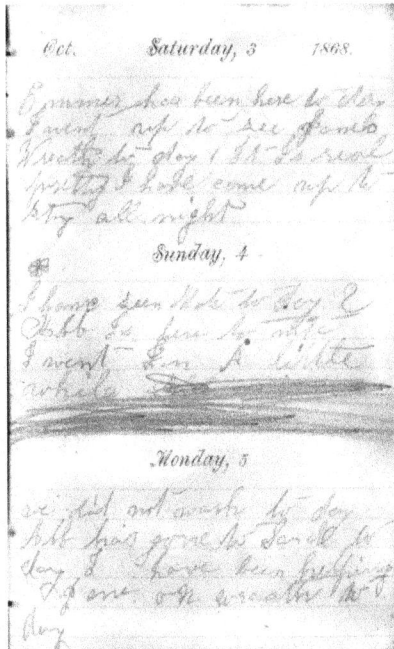

October, Tuesday 6, 1868
I have been helping Jane again today.

October, Wednesday 7, 1868
have been helping Jane again on her wreath. I staid all night
to Pa's last night.

October, Thursday 8, 1868
Lafa came down here and she dropped a pail of ----. It slip out
of her hand and knocked her over.

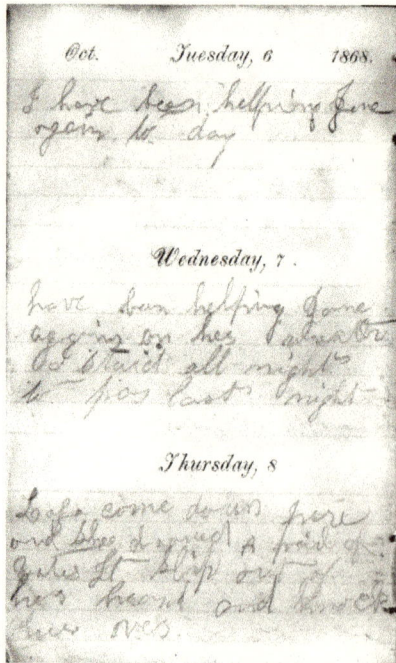

October, Friday 9, 1868
Velma has put her wreath together today. Lina and Lafa has been here today. we churned this evening and real tired.

October, Saturday 10, 1868
Ma, Pa, Aunt Lizzie & Minnie come last night about 12. Ma brought me a cushion of beads. Aunt Lizzie, Minnie is here. Jane finished her wreath today.

October, Sunday 11, 1868
Abb is nott here and It has been awful lonesome to have been to meeting twice. Oh dear I don't know what I should do. It is so lonesome.

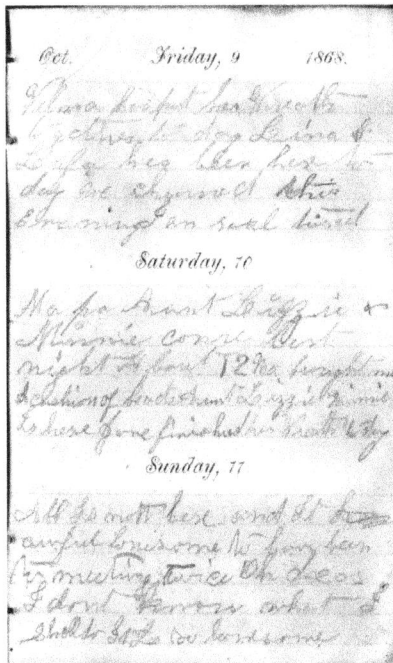

October, Monday 12, 1868
we have been a-washing today. I have been to the post office today.

October, Tuesday 13, 1868
I have been to the post office. I do wish that Abb would come home because it has been so darned lonesome.

October, Wednesday 14, 1868
have not been to the post office today.

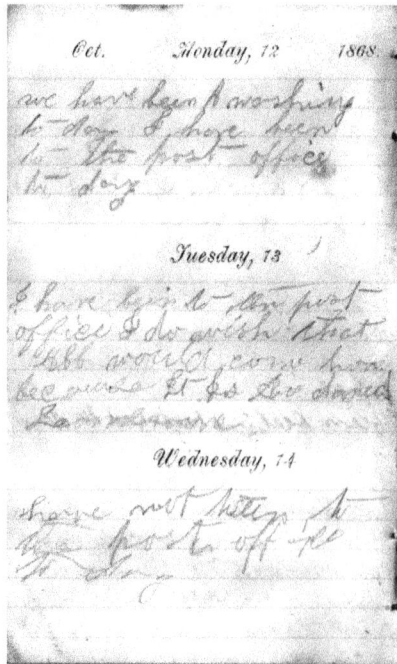

October, Thursday 15, 1868
did not go to the post office. Jane went. Abb has come home. I am glad but I feel bad enough if he has come.

October, Friday 16, 1868
been to meeting. Abb come home with Jane. she dared me to ask him if he was going to be married. I did. I have been feeling real bad today. ~~have seen Abb.~~

October, Saturday 17, 1868
we have churned today. George has cut him. the girls went up to Mrs. Whitney's. have not seen Abb today - but can't help it if I ------.

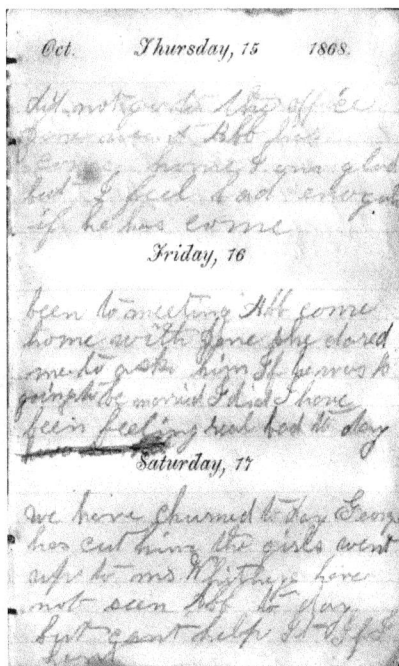

October, Sunday 18, 1868
have been to meeting 2 today. Come home with Abb and Jane. went in when they was quiet awhile. Abb said if I would come where he was he would kiss me.

October, Monday 19, 1868
Abb, Jerome, & Ed has gone to the Institute. It has reind [rained] today. It is lonesome. I went to Mrs. Clark's today. ----- ---- -------- Abb------ --- --.

October, Tuesday 20, 1868
Sarah, Aunt Mary, Aunt Lucy, Jennie went up to Aunt Harriet's today. Orion carried them up. It is darned lonesome but can't help it.

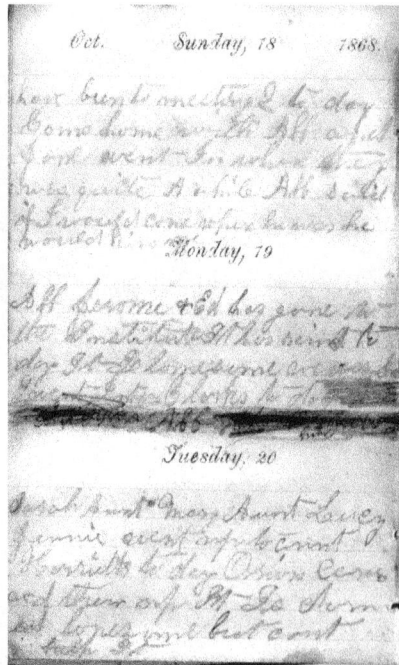

October, Wednesday 21, 1868
we have churned today. It has been raining. It is lonesome.
Orion is plowing. have not been at the post office today.

October, Thursday 22, 1868
did not go enywheres today. It is real lonesome since Abb and
Jerome went away.

October, Friday 23, 1868
went up to Cyrus's all day. going to stay all night.

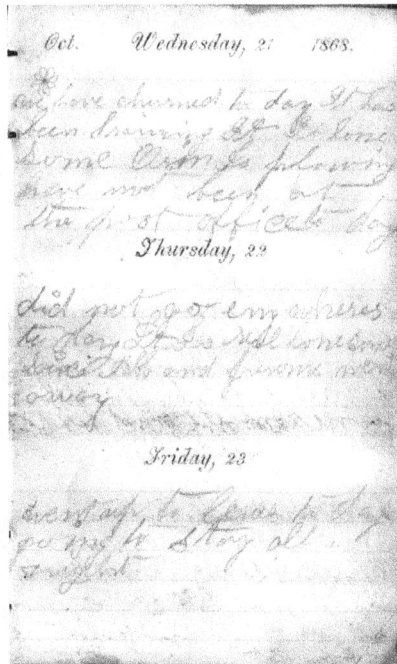

October, Saturday 24, 1868
have been to Uncle Cyrus a-visiting today. had a good visit.

October, Sunday 25, 1868
Staid to Uncle Philander's last night. went over to Mrs. Porters. I come home today. It is real lonesome. Abb is not here tonight.

October, Monday 26, 1868
I come over to Uncle John's to work. I cried just as hard as I could because I had to come.

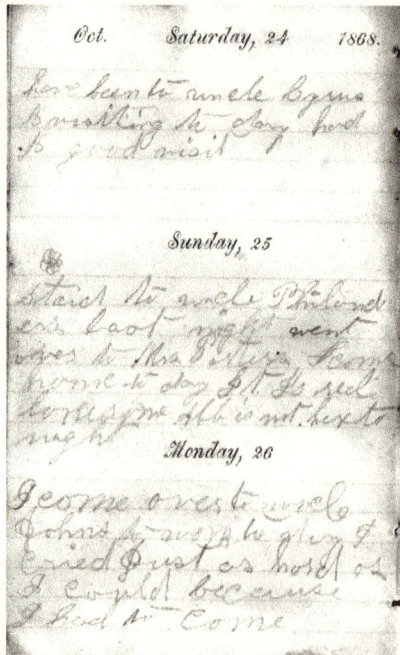

October, Tuesday 27, 1868
It is awful lonesome. Ellie Pritchard came to make me a visit but did not stay because I was over here and went back home.

October, Wednesday 28, 1868
It has been real lonesome today. Jane & Sarah come over here and staid the evening. I have been knitting. I am tired.

October, Thursday 29, 1868
have got through. went up to Pa's this afternoon. Ellie was there.

October, Friday 30, 1868
The girls has gone to Cortland. Helen has been here. have been up to the post office.

October, Saturday 31, 1868
they got back today. Jane and i went to meeting but did not stay. got my apron. seen Abb today.

November, Sunday 1, 1868
went to meeting twice today. Abb is here tonight. I sit by the stove and Abb put his hand into my pocket and got my butternuts.

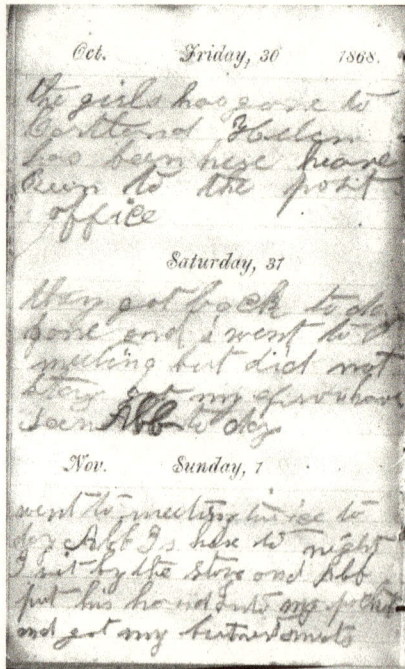

November, Monday 2, 1868

have been washing today. have not been to the post office. hain't heard from Vel today but spose she'll get along.

November, Tuesday 3, 1868

Lib, Line, Maria, & Oscar is here today. Is Election Day. A good ell [election] going on. have been to Clark's 2 today.

November, Wednesday 4, 1868

have been butchering. Frank, Hut, Pritchard, Aunt Hattie, Aunt Lizzie and Abb is here to night. have got a cold.

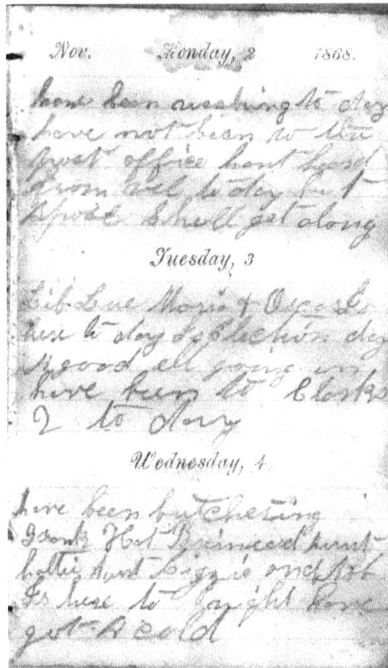

November, Thursday 5, 1868
Julius come back today. Vel has been here. have been to the post office today. Jane has been to Pritchards. have seen Abb today.

November, Friday 6, 1868
have not been to the post office today, but have see Abb. he come down after some citrons.

November, Saturday 7, 1868
Jane and I went to the store. Abb was helping Uncle Chauncey move his building. he was driving [the] horse.

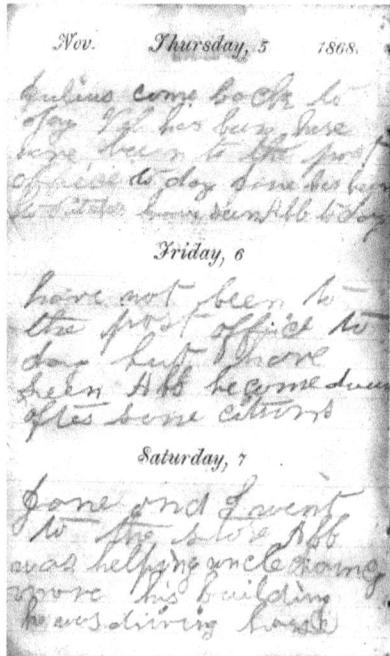

November, Sunday 8, 1868

Osphia [Sophia] has come today with Jerome. Abb is here tonight. I went in when i come out. i went around to them all and told them something. ~~I kissed Abb once and he kissed me twice.~~

November, Monday 9, 1868

I did not sleep enough to stick in a pig's ear. went down stairs with Abb when he went home. Osphia [Sophia] has gone to-day. Jerome went to his school. it has rained all day.

November, Tuesday 10, 1868

it has been raining all day. been Cleaning upstairs today. have not see Abb. Aunt Em has got a boy 3 months old but I can't help it.

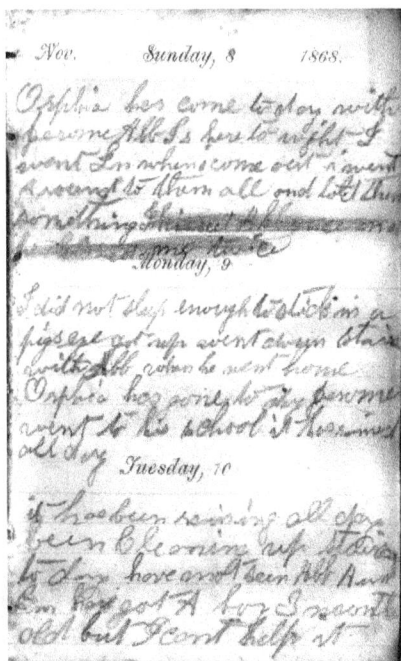

November, Wednesday 11, 1868
Went up to Pa's this evening to see Aunt Lizzie & Minnie. had a good time. I saw Abb there too. I written a Letter to Em.

November, Thursday 12, 1868
I dreamt last night that Abb come home with me. have not see Abb today. Vel, Lafa, & Herbie was down here tonight.

November, Friday 13, 1868
Velma come down this evening to have me go up to Mrs. Osborn's. I went. had a good time. went to Pa's to stay all night. have not seen Abb tonight.

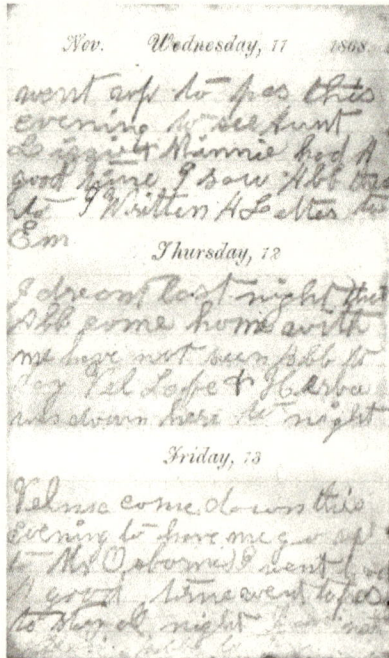

November, Saturday 14, 1868
have not been doing much today.

November, Sunday 15, 1868
went to meeting 2 today. this evening Abb is here. ==== === ====
=I went in --- ------ -----there.

November, Monday 16, 1868
we washed this morning. School commenced today. went to
the post office tonight.

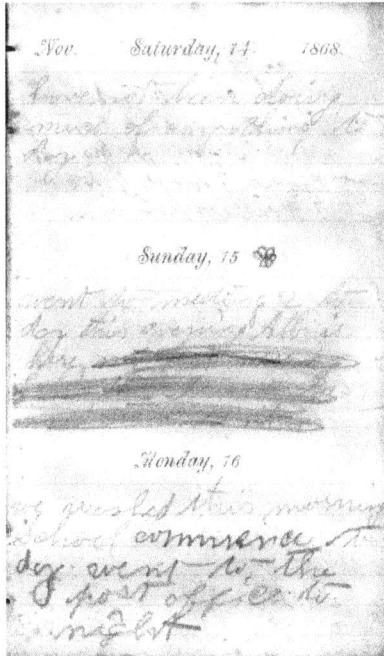

November, Tuesday 17, 1868
have been to school today. like the teacher very well. ~~Abb come home ---- -- ----yesterday.~~

November, Wednesday 18, 1868
have been to school today. went to the post office but did not get enything.

November, Thursday 19, 1868
went to school today. It has rained most all day. did not go to the post office.

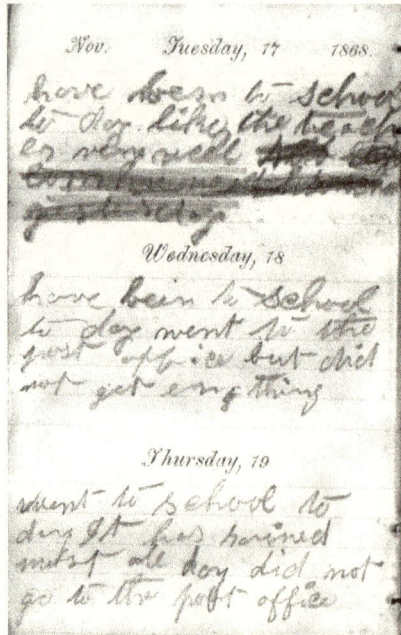

November, Friday 20, 1868
have been to school today. Greene and Oren went to the Exhibition. Jerome come home tonight. went to the post office 3 times today.

November, Saturday 21, 1868
went to meeting 2 today. My fingers feel pretty bad. Mr. Ensign, Mrs. Ensign here tonight.

November, Sunday 22, 1868
have been to meeting twice today. Abb is here today. He looks as natural as ever.

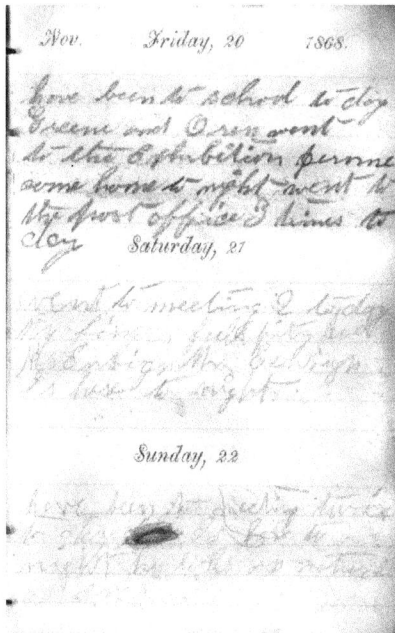

November, Monday 23, 1868
have been to school today.

November, Tuesday 24, 1868
have been to school today. my fingers is bout the same.

November, Wednesday 25, 1868
went to Dozsten's funrel today. Mate went down today with
me afterward.

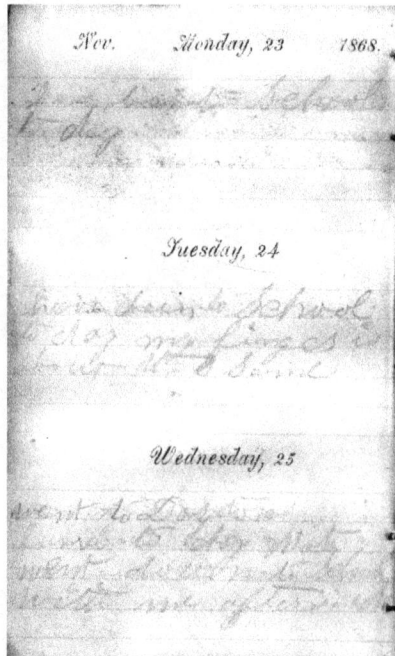

November, Thursday 26, 1868
today is Thanksgiving day and school does not keep [hours].
It rains today.

November, Friday 27, 1868
I went to school today.

November, Saturday 28, 1868
It Is kind a lonesome. I had my fingers opened today.

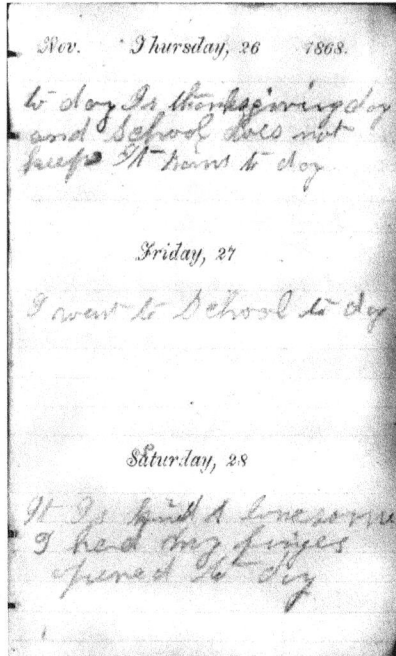

November, Sunday 29, 1868
have not been to meeting today but am a-going this Evening.

November, Monday 30, 1868
we washed today. I went to school.

D**ecember, Tuesday 1, 1868**
I went to school today.

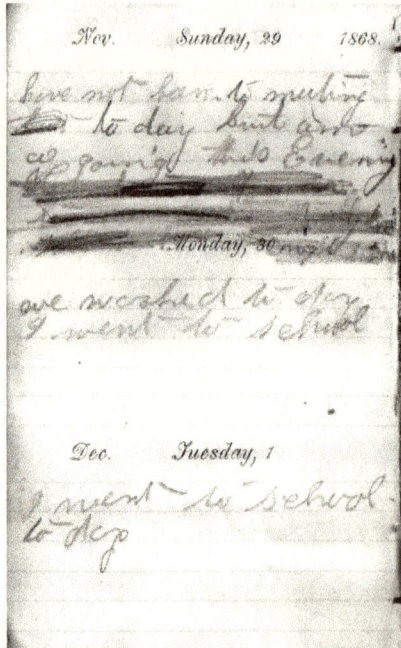

December, Wednesday 2, 1868
have been to school.

December, Thursday 3, 1868
I went to school. had lots of fun.

December, Friday 4, 1868
have been to school today.

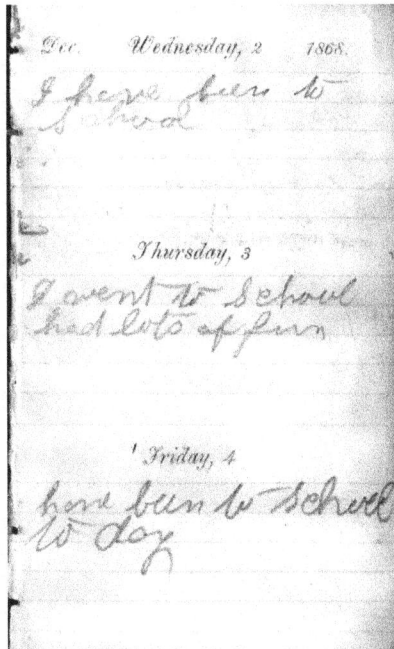

December, Saturday 5, 1868

Arose this morning and found considerable amount of snow on the ground. has been snowing all day. looks as if mighty fine sleighing. had my hair cut.

December, Sunday 6, 1869

I did not go to Church today, but went this Evening.

December, Monday 7, 1868

I went to school today. I had to carry my dinner it stormed so bad.

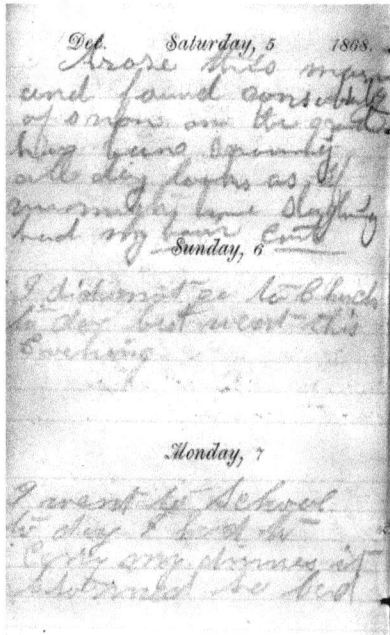

December, Tuesday 8, 1868

I carried my dinner today. there was not many scholars to-day.

December, Wednesday 9, 1868

It is quite pleasant today. i went to school today. Mary Wise staid here last night.

December, Thursday 10, 1868

I went to school. it is storming some today.

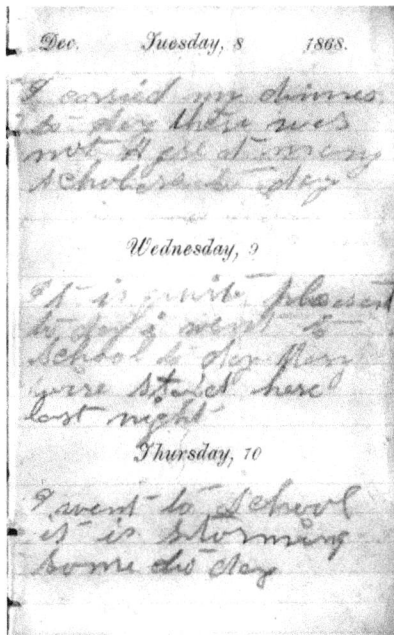

December, Friday 11, 1868
we spoke peices today. it is quite pleasant today.

December, Saturday 12, 1868
It is quite cold today. hain't been doing much of enything today.

December, Sunday 13, 1868
have been to meeting 2 today. Abb come home with Jane and they have gone upstairs.

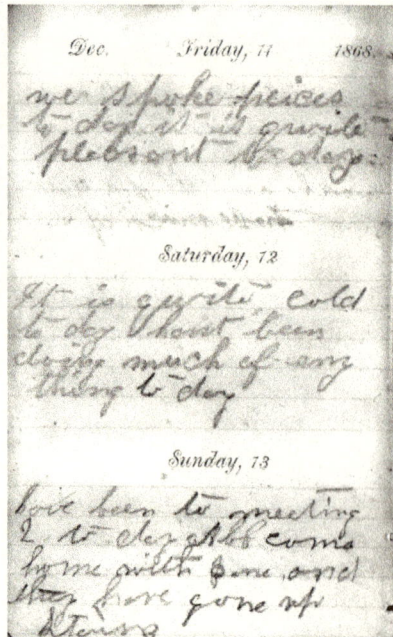

December, Monday 14, 1868
A~~-- ---- ------~~. I have been to school today. we did not wash eny today. did not have much of eny fun.

December, Tuesday 15, 1868
I went to school today. had lots of fun today.

December, Wednesday 16, 1868
have been at school today. Am a-going to Donations tonight.

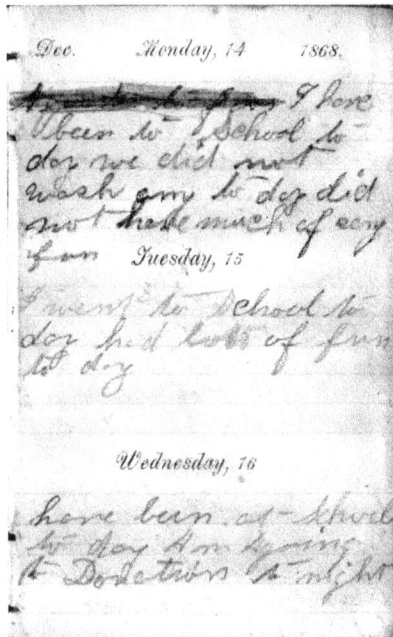

December, Thursday 17, 1868
went to Donations last night and had a real good time. === ===
=== ==== ==== ===== had lots of fun.

December, Friday 18, 1868
I went to school today but did not have to stay at noon and
got my lessons - they all look real sleepy.

December, Saturday 19, 1868
have not been doing much of enything. went up to Mrs. Holmes' last night. had a real good time. Abb took --- ------.

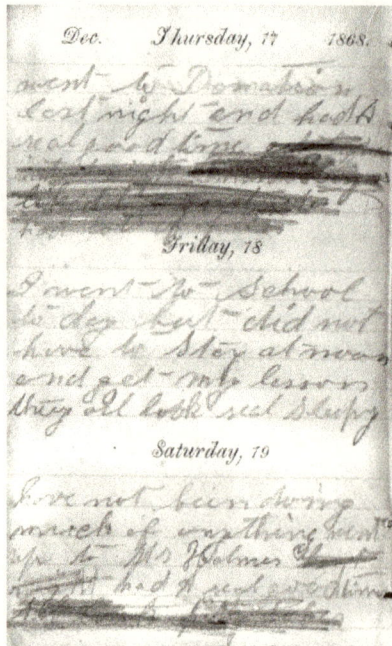

December, Sunday 20, 1868
have been to meeting. took a walk just before dusk. Jane and I went to meeting tonight. ~~Abb ---- as far --- --- they ate first ---- ---- ---.~~

December, Monday 21, 1868
we have washed today. Jane, Sarah and George has gone up on Potter Hill. It is lonesome. went to school.

December, Tuesday 22, 1868
I went to school today. Jane and the rest has got back.

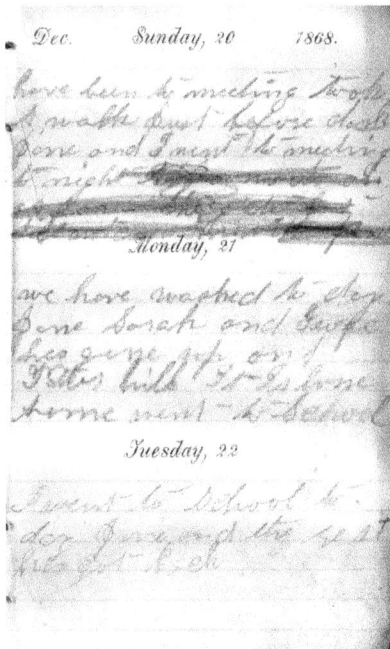

December, Wednesday 23, 1868
I did not go to school today but staid home and worked on my new dress.

December, Thursday 24, 1868
I went to school today. hung up my stocking tonight.

December, Friday 25, 1868
I went up to Pa's. Ma gave me a Christmas present. 3 pictures, a pair of sleeve buttons, and a Bible and lots of other things.

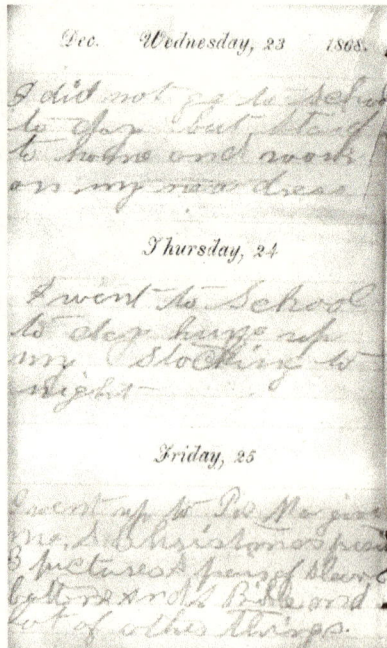

December, Saturday 26, 1868

I caught cold yesterday. ~~Abb ---- last night. ---- ---- them so me and ---- ---- he kissed ---- and some --- -- --.~~

December, Sunday 27, 1868

Mr. Philips and his wife have come. ~~Abb --- has --- ------ --- ---- ----.~~

December, Monday 28, 1868

~~Abb ----- this morning. Abb come --- - - -----. I give him a kiss ---- for it.~~

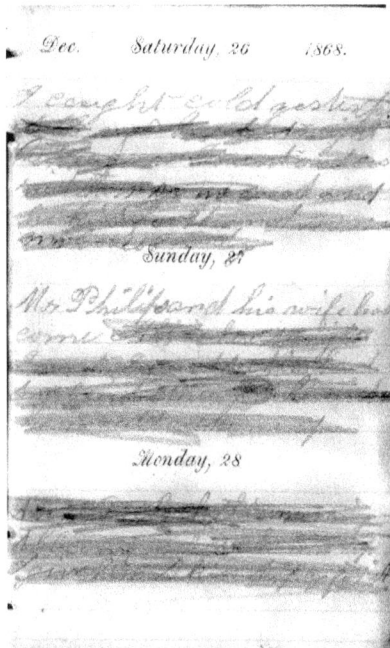

December, Tuesday 29, 1868
[No entry.]

December, Wednesday 30, 1868
[No entry.]

December, Thursday 31, 1868
[No entry.]

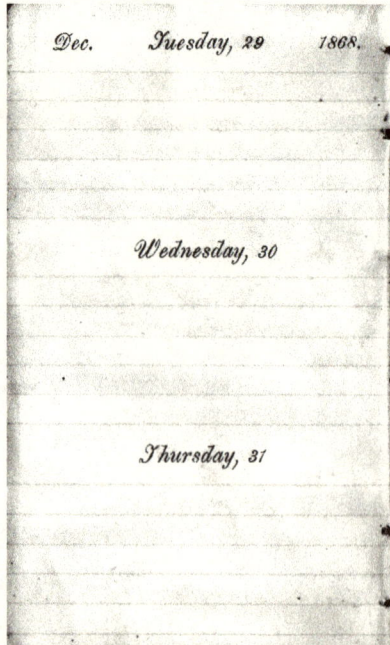

Then Lucy started 1869 by writing over the top of the 1868 entries.....

January, Sunday 10, 1869 I went to Church today. Jane has gone off to bed for she hain't any wheres around.

January, Monday 11, 1869
we washed today but did not hang out our clothes. I went to school. It is not very pleasant.

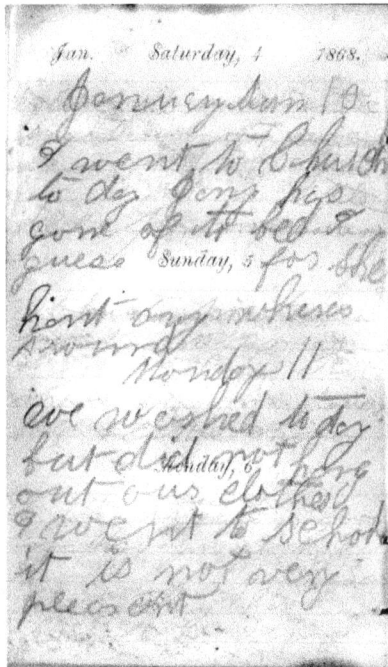

January, Tuesday 12, 1869

I arose this morning - it is really pleasant. Went to school.

January, Wednesday 13, 1869

i did not go to school this forenoon but went this afternoon.

January, Thursday 14, 1869

arose this morning and found that it was real pleasant. went to school today.

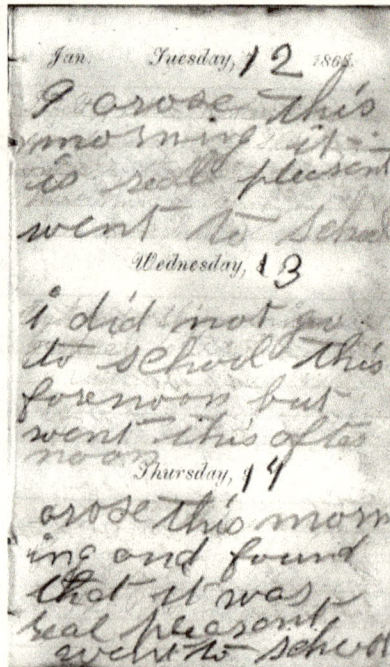

January, Friday 15, 1869
did not go to School this forenoon but went this afternoon.

January, Saturday 16, 1869
Ma has been here today to make a visit to Jones's. Magazines come today.

January, Sunday 17, 1869
went to meeting twice today. Aunt Mary, Aunt Lucy, Uncle Noel has gone up to Uncle Amos.

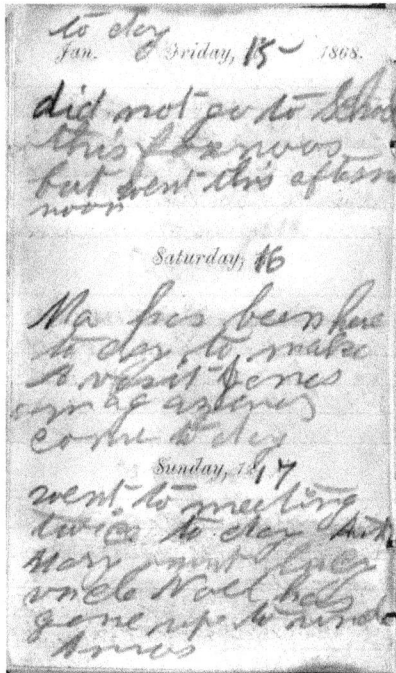

January, Monday 18, 1869
I did not go to school this forenoon but went this afternoon.
had a good time.

January, Tuesday 19, 1869
Ensign's donations is tonight. I had an invitation but did not
go. Went to school today.

~~**January, Wednesday 20, 1869**~~
~~have been ------twice today - have had some fun this evening.~~

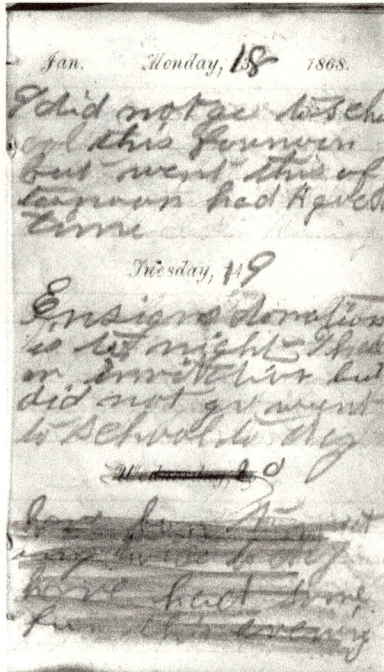

January, Wednesday 20, 1869
Went up to stay all night with ------ last night.

January, Thursday 21, 1869
i have been to School today.

January, Friday 22, 1869
went to ~~School~~ Mrs. McLaughlin's last night. got home after 2.

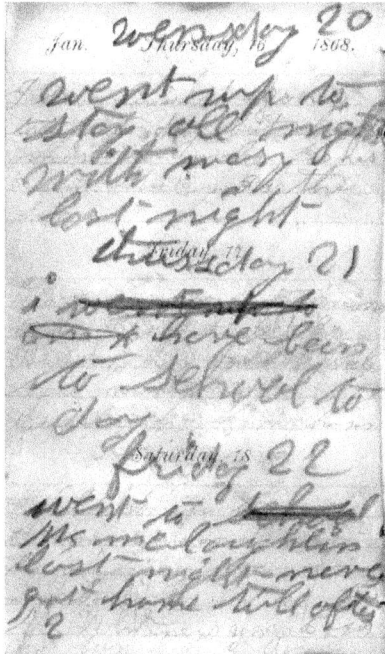

January, Saturday 23, 1869
have not been doing much of anything.

January, Sunday 24, 1869
I have been to meeting twice today. ~~Abb and~~ I guess that Jane
has gone to bed.

January, Monday 25, 1869
Staid to home and help wash but went [to school] this afternoon.

January, Tuesday 26, 1869
i went to school today have had lots of fun.

January, Wednesday 27, 1869
Arose this morning very early and found it pleasant. have been to School today.

January, Thursday 28, 1869
i did not have much fun today. have been to school - snowballed me.

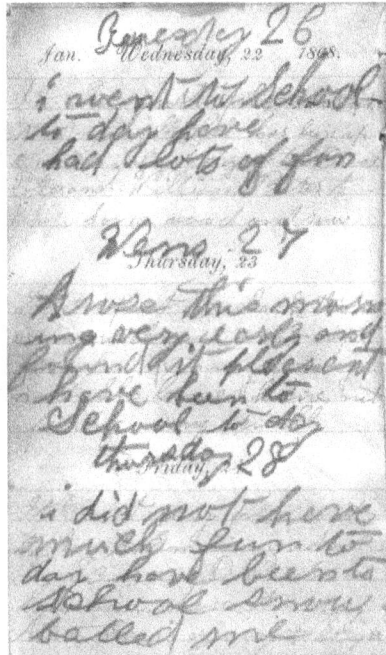

January, Friday 29, 1869
have been down to Lower Cincinattus tonight - had a rousing
good time.

What happened to them?

BOWEN, Amos, 1808-1883, married to Phylinda Potter, son of Amos & Elsie (Seamans) Bowen.

BOWEN, Phylinda, wife of Amos, died 1900, around age 85, daughter of Charles & Paulina (Carver) Potter Sr.

CHATFIELD, George died 1884, age 28.

CHATFIELD, Mary, wife of Curtis, died 1894, age 70.

CLARK, [Abb] Albert Frank, 1846-1923, married first to Lucy's cousin Jane Seamans, then to Lucy's friend Lizzie Rockwell.

CLARK, Elizabeth, second wife of Albert F., 1853-1937 daughter of Ira & Hannah (Beebe) Rockwell.

HUTCHINSON, Velma [Potter] 1852 - 1899 married Andrew Hutchinson; children: Edward A., Richard D., De Forrest, Harley, Albert Hutchinson.

POTTER, Edmund, 1830 - 1906, son of Hardin & Ruth (Champion) Potter. Married three times - first to Lillis (mother of Lucy) then to Jane Halbert, then to Mrs. Hattie Chatfield. He was educated in the common schools and learned the trade of blacksmith - for some years employed by Kingman, Sturtevant & Larabie in the carriage business, as a blacksmith. For twenty years, was postmaster of Taylor. He held the office of justice of the peace many years. He was an expert penman and used to give lessons in penmanship. He was a member of the Wesleyan Methodist Church.

POTTER, Herbert 1861 - ?, employed as a blacksmith, railroad worker, and eventually had his own trucking business. He was a communicant of the Methodist Episcopal Church. He married Alice M. Allen of Taylor. Children: Waldo Roscoe and Vivian Ruth.

POTTER, Jane, second wife of Edmund, died 1899, age 73, daughter of Seth & Sophia Halbert.

POTTER, Lafa [Lafrenza], died 1893, age 33, daughter of Edmund & Lillis (Cole) Potter.

POTTER, Lillis, first wife of Edmund, died 1861, age 29 after giving birth to son Herbert - daughter of Newell & Susan (Potter) Cole.

POTTER, Lucy Jane, died Sept 25, 1874, age 19 years 6 months 2 days, daughter of Edmund & Lillis (Cole) Potter.

SEAMANS, Jane, wife of Abb [Albert] Clark, died 1874, age 28, daughter of Noel and Lucy (Potter) Seamans.

SEAMANS, Jerome, a teacher, died 1871, age 31, son of Noel and Lucy (Potter) Seamans.

SEAMANS, Lucy, wife of Noel, died 1887, age 79, daughter of Charles & Paulina (Carver) Potter.

SEAMANS, Noel, died 1872, age 75. Married to Lucy Potter, son of Jonathan & Sarah (Bowen) Seamans.

SHUFELT, George W., 1834-1888, son of Henry & Sally (Taylor) Shufelt, wife's name was Amy.

Afterward

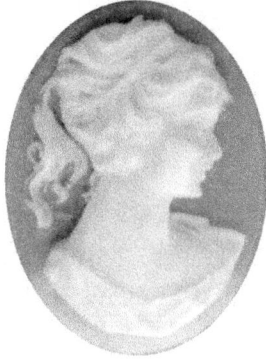

Lucy Jane Potter died just five and a half years from her last entry in this diary on September 25, 1874 at the age of nineteen.

Before her death, her beloved Abb married her cousin Jane. Jane also died in 1874, three months before Lucy. Abb's second wife was Lucy's good friend Lizzie (Elizabeth) Rockwell.

Lucy is buried a half-mile from her aunt's house,
in the Taylor Rural Cemetery behind the Taylor
Wesleyan Church on Route 26, four miles north
of Cincinnatus, New York.

Bibliography

Vickery, Judson. "Taylor Rural Cemetery A-K." Rootsweb. Accessed October 21, 2008 <http://files.usgwarchives.org/ny/cortland/cemeteries/taylorrural-ak.txt>.

Vickery, Judson. "Taylor Rural Cemetery L-Z." Rootsweb. Accessed October 21, 2008 <http://files.usgwarchives.org/ny/cortland/cemeteries/taylorrural-lz.txt>.

Crankshaw. David C. "Taylor Rural Cemetery ." 1986. Rootsweb. Accessed October 21, 2008 <http://www.rootsweb.ancestry.com/~nycortla/taylorc/taylor.txt>.

VanCleave, Suzanne. "RootsWeb: RIGENWEB." June, 25, 2004. Rootsweb. Accessed April 15, 2009 <http://listsearches.rootsweb.com/th/read/RIGENWEB/2004-06/1088291909>.

More books from NYHR Press

My Story -
A Year in the Life of a Country Girl

My Centennial Diary -
A Year in the Life of a Country Boy